ArtScroll History Series®

Rabbi Nosson Scherman / Rabbi Meir Zlotowitz

General Editors

by
Sarah Wahrman

Published by
Mesorah Publications, ltd

NEVER DIES

A Survivor's Tale

FIRST EDITION
First Impression … May 1999

Published and Distributed by
MESORAH PUBLICATIONS, LTD.
4401 Second Avenue / Brooklyn, N.Y 11232

Distributed in Europe by
J. LEHMANN HEBREW BOOKSELLERS
20 Cambridge Terrace
Gateshead, Tyne and Wear
England NE8 1RP

Distributed in Israel by
SIFRIATI / A. GITLER
10 Hashomer Street
Bnei Brak 51361

Distributed in Australia and New Zealand by
GOLDS BOOK & GIFT SHOP
36 William Street
Balaclava 3183, Vic., Australia

Distributed in South Africa by
KOLLEL BOOKSHOP
Shop 8A Norwood Hypermarket
Norwood 2196, Johannesburg, South Africa

Typography by CompuScribe at ArtScroll Studios, Ltd.

Printed in the United States of America by Noble Book Press Corp.
Bound by Sefercraft, Quality Bookbinders, Ltd., Brooklyn N.Y. 11232

Letter of Approbation from
HaRav Pinchas Hirschsprung ז״ל
Chief Rabbi of Montreal

הסכמת הרב הגאון מוהר״ר פנחס הירשפרונג זצ״ל
ראש הרבנים במונטריאל

ב״ה

הנני בזה להגיד לאדם ישרו ה״ה הרב הגאון המפורסם חו״ב בכל
חדרי תורה מ׳ שלמה וואהרמאן שליט״א חובר חבורים מחוכמים וכבר
הדפיס חמשה חבורים אשר ראהו גדולים ושבחוהו.

כעת הודיע לי על דבר רעיתו שתחי׳ שחשקה נפשה להוציא לאור
את זכרונותיה מימי המלחמה ולהדפיס מה שעשו הנאצים ימ״ש
לאחב״י, ואע״פ שכבר נדפס קצת מה זה שעשה אותו העמלק ימ״ש.
– דבר זה מצוה מדאורייתא לקיים זכור את אשר עשה לך עמלק
ובעל יין מצולה הדפיס ג״כ אודות זה (על הגזירות הנוראות שנגזרו על
היהודים בשנת ת״ח).

ולזאת חוב קדוש לספר למען ידעו הדורות הבאים את מעשה
התעתועים של הנאצים ימ״ש והעולם כולו ידעו מזה ולא עשו שום
מחאה.

הבה ונקוה כי הקב״ה ינקום את נקמתנו וישלם להנאצים שתהי׳ להם
מפלה במהרה דידן – אמן.

פנחס הירשפרונג

עש״ק פ׳ חיי שרה תשנ״א לפ״ק

✍ Table of Contents

✍ **Introduction:**   xi
ZACHOR — REMEMBER
The Halachic Response to the Holocaust
A Personal Memoir

✍ **Acknowledgments:**   xix

✍ **Chapter 1:**   23
CZECHOSLOVAKIA BEFORE WORLD WAR II
Anti-Semitism in Czechoslovakia

✍ **Chapter 2:**   27
GROWING UP IN A TIME OF UPHEAVAL
My Education — Both in School and Out / Shattered Dreams /
The Situation Becomes More Grave / A New Vocation

✍ **Chapter 3:**   43
LEAVING HOME
Our Attempts to Escape the War Machine

✍ **Chapter 4:**   52
THE NAZIS ARRIVE
Arrival at Auschwitz / Another Move / Return to Auschwitz

✍ **Chapter 5:**   81
GUBEN AND BERGEN-BELSEN
Death March / Bergen-Belsen

Chapter 6:   **107**
LIBERATION
The Nazis Surrender

Chapter 7:   **126**
RECOVERY IN SWEDEN
New Friends / What of My Own Family? / New Family /
More Family News

Chapter 8:   **165**
A NEW LIFE
The Importance of a Haven / Learning From the Past

Chapter 9:   **174**
DID ANYONE REALLY CARE?
A Halachic View / The Nations of the World

Chapter 10:   **187**
LIKE SHEEP TO THE SLAUGHTER?
Courage and Heroism in the Ghettos

Glossary: **197**

INTRODUCTION:
ZACHOR — REMEMBER

"Remember what Amalek did unto you on the way, as you came out of Egypt . Do not forget it" "זְכוֹר אֵת אֲשֶׁר עָשָׂה לְךָ עֲמָלֵק בַּדֶּרֶךְ בְּצֵאתְכֶם מִמִּצְרָיִם...לֹא תִשְׁכָּח" (*Devarim* 25:17-19). This mandate is one of the 613 *mitzvos* of the Torah.

This *mitzvah* of *Zachor*, then, was my motivation for writing this book. As early as the 1950s, my husband's mentor, Hagaon Harav Eliezer Silver of Cincinnati, had urged him to recount his personal experiences in the Nazi inferno, in compliance with the *mitzvah* of remembering the evil deeds of the Amalekites. He quoted the opinion of the Vilna Gaon that Germany had the possible status of Amalek. I now feel that it is also my solemn duty to publish a book on the subject.

It has always been part of the Jewish tradition to respond to the changes in our long history with introspection. For example, after the expulsion of the Jews from Spain in 1492, Harav Yosef Ya'avetz wrote the *Or Hachaim* and Harav Yehudah Ibn

Virga wrote *Shevet Yehudah*. After the pogroms during the Cossack revolt in 1648, Harav Nosson Nota Hanover wrote *Yeven Metzulah*.

Our generation has suffered a great tragedy, the murder of six million of our people. The systematic development of a sophisticated murder apparatus employing all of the 20th century's advances in science and technology proves that this was more than a mere moral lapse. It was a coldly calculated project grounded in a philosophy expounded by a nation of savages who dedicated all of their intellectual talents and technological prowess to its success.

All this, despite the fact that the Germans prided themselves on being the foremost representative of enlightenment and progress. Theirs was a culture based on ethics and morals. Their moral and religious standards demanded unlimited love of one's fellowman.

The German nation took pride in its contribution to the development of art, music, and humanism. It viewed itself as a nation of superior culture, a nation that had given much to the world. And yet, this purportedly "superior" nation sank to the levels of bestiality never before seen in the history of mankind. With all its "love" of humanity, this so-called German culture-ethic became translated into a virulent hatred of Jews and the cultivation of torture and murder of entire communities. This same culture-ethic of "love" of humanity became the perfect satanic vehicle, encouraging its proponents to bring about the most comprehensive genocide in history.

The German people, together with other nations who eagerly joined the genocide project, exhibited extreme dedication and frightful consistency in the practical execution of their abominable project until its bitter end. Their commitment to devastation was more consistent than their commitment to culture.

In times of trial and tribulation nothing is more natural for observant Jews than to turn to our traditional response: looking at ourselves, our deeds and misdeeds, our faith and our world.

Halachah definitely demands such a response. It must, however, be emphasized that to completely understand the meaning and significance of the Holocaust may be beyond human capabilities. We must, therefore, discard any thought of knowing that which is ultimately beyond human understanding.

After Hashem forgave the Israelites for making the golden calf, Moshe Rabbeinu asked, "Hashem, please reveal your glory to me" — "הַרְאֵנִי נָא אֶת כְּבֹדֶךָ" (*Shemos* 33:18). Hashem responded, "You will see My back, but My face may not be seen" — "וְרָאִיתָ אֶת אֲחֹרָי וּפָנַי לֹא יֵרָאוּ" (*Shemos* 33:23). The Midrash explains that Hashem was telling Moshe that a person, as part of this world *(lefanai),* cannot fully comprehend events that are intellectually perplexing and emotionally troubling. Only after this world and its history will have been completed *(achorai)* will the enigma of Hashem's will be fully understood.

WHAT SHOULD OUR RESPONSE BE? MAIMONIDES

The Halachic Response to the Holocaust teaches: "When a tragedy occurs, one must not pass it off as the way of the world, but rather, we must assume that it was due to sins. Consequently, it should become a stimulus to repentance. We must search our deeds and correct our shortcomings" (*Maimonides*, Chapter 1: *Laws of the Fasts*).

However, the Gaon Harav Aharon Soloveitchik points out that although we must attribute tragedy to sin, we dare not point an accusing finger at anyone but ourselves. *Pirkei Avos* teaches us that on the public level there is an obligation to judge *Klal Yisrael* as a whole only in a favorable manner. There is no license to impute transgressions to the Jewish people nor to blame them for what happened (*Midrash Yelamdeinu: Shoftim,* Chapter 6).

Similarly, in 1977 the Gaon Harav Yitzchok Hutner was quoted in the *Jewish Observer* saying that we have no right to interpret the events of the *churban* of European Jewry as any

R' Aharon Soloveitchik   *R' Yitzchok Hutner*

kind of punishment for specific sins. One would have to be a prophet or a Talmudic sage to claim knowledge of the specific reasons for what befell us. Anyone on a lesser plane who claims to do so tramples on the bodies of the *kedoshim* who died *al kiddush Hashem* and misuses the power to interpret and understand Jewish history.

When Hagaon Harav Eliezer Silver was asked to explain the meaning of the Holocaust, he simply replied, "The ways of Hashem are concealed from us" — "דַּרְכֵי ד' נִסְתָּרִים." He utterly condemned any attempt to point an accusing finger or to place responsibility for this catastrophe squarely on anyone's shoulders.

When the prophet Yeshayahu debased the Jewish people by declaring, "I dwell among a people with impure lips" — "וּבְתוֹךְ עַם טְמֵא שְׂפָתַיִם אָנֹכִי יוֹשֵׁב" (*Yeshayahu* 6:5), it was considered a most grievous sin, which required atonement and vindication. Rashi comments that the severity of Yeshayahu's sin was due to the fact that there was no Divine command (in the form of a prophecy) that charged Yeshayahu to decry the Jews as a people; nor was this an attempt to admonish them for the purpose of improving their spiritual comportment. It was rather an accusatory statement against his fellow Jews, made of Yeshayahu's own volition (*Yevamos* 49b).

No Jewish leader, continued Harav Silver, is granted license to downgrade his own people. To debase the religious charac-

From left to right: the Boyaner Rebbe, R' Eliezer Silver, the Kopyczynitzer Rebbe

ter of the Holocaust's victims by suggesting that their destruction was an inevitable result of specific sins they committed is not only an unproved theory, but it is quite cruel. One does not dare to tarnish the memory of the six million *kedoshim* in such a treacherous manner, concluded Harav Silver.

From a *halachic* perspective, there is no adequate explanation any mortal can offer with any amount of certainty for the sins that caused the Holocaust. The ways of the Almighty are hidden from us. Thus, the approach of ascribing and imputing transgressions to those martyrs who died *al kiddush Hashem* is totally inconsistent with the Torah viewpoint. However, one dare not attribute the tragic events of such enormity merely to chance, to historical inevitability. Our sages taught us long ago: "No man bruises his finger here on earth, unless it was so decreed against him in Heaven" — ״אֵין אָדָם נוֹקֵף אֶצְבָּעוֹ מִלְמַטָה אֶלָּא אִם כֵּן מַכְרִיזִין עָלָיו מִלְמַעְלָה״ (*Chullin* 7b). Nothing ever occurs in the universe without the full will and consent of Hashem. The eminent Gaon of Dvinsk, Harav Meir Simchah HaKohen, in his classic *sefer Meshech Chochmah*, refers

R' Meir Simchah HaKohen – author of
Ohr Somayach and Meshech Chochmah

to the words of the prophet Yirmiyah, "To You (Hashem) nations will come from the ends of the earth and say: 'It was all falsehood that our ancestors inherited, futility that has no purpose! Can a man make gods for himself? – They are not gods!'" — "אַךְ שֶׁקֶר נָחֲלוּ אֲבוֹתֵינוּ הֶבֶל וְאֵין בָּם מוֹעִיל - הֲיַעֲשֶׂה לּוֹ אָדָם אֱלֹקִים וְהֵמָּה לֹא אֱלֹקִים" (*Yirmiyah* 16:19-20). Harav Meir Simchah foresaw the search for false gods. He saw that many a Jew would altogether forget his heritage and would be considered a new, inexperienced citizen in the false world of culture. He would then leave the study of his own law to study languages that do not belong to him. He would learn from the worthless rather than from the worthwhile.

Harav Meir Simchah continues, "Do not rejoice, O Israel, and do not exult like the people!" — "אַל תִּשְׂמַח יִשְׂרָאֵל אֶל גִּיל כָּעַמִּים" (*Hoshea* 9:1). "Then will come a rushing stormwind, uprooting him from his source, carrying him to a distant nation whoselanguage he has not learned. Then he will know that he is a stanger ... that his heritage is the root of Israel and his consolations are those of Hashem's prophets who prophesied about the son of Yishai at the end of days."

It must be remembered that Harav Meir Simchah lived in the years just prior to the Holocaust. His book, *Meshech Chochmah,* was published in 1927, six years before Hitler's rise to power. Therefore, he certainly was not pointing an accusing finger at any victims of the Holocaust by theologically rationalizing such an incomprehensible tragedy. Harav Meir Simchah was merely offering a logical and historical explanation for why such a tragedy might well occur in the future, and in so doing, he was expressing Torah views. The Torah itself is replete with admonitions of potential tragedy if we fail to hearken to the words of Hashem. Such calamities are specifically enumerated, and in great detail, in the two *tochachos* found in the Torah. The concept of reward and punishment is listed among Maimonides' 13 articles of the Jewish faith. Our reaction must be, as Maimonides teaches, to follow the path of *teshuvah* and constantly strive for spiritual improvement. We must be aware of our role as Jews and strengthen our observance of all aspects of the Torah.

THIS WORK IS NOT INTENDED TO BE A DOCUMENTARY of the events of the Nazi period. It is, rather, a narrative com-

A Personal Memoir posed of personal experiences during those dark days. The events related here were those I witnessed and participated in as a youngster, and they are recorded now, some 54 years later, without the benefit of any diary or memorandum. To supplement these memories and to place events into proper perspective, I have relied on some excellent documentary histories published on the Holocaust.

When the *Kohen Gadol*, the High Priest in the *Beis Hamidkash* in Jerusalem, completed the Yom Kippur service in the Holy of Holies, he proceeded to read several relevant chapters from the Torah and then announced, "More than I have read before you, is written here" — "יוֹתֵר מִמַּה שֶׁקָּרָאתִי לִפְנֵיכֶם כָּתוּב כָּאן" (*Yoma* 68b). In a similar vein, I would like to state that much more than I have written here occurred there. It is humanly impossible to describe the horror in its totality. This work has barely scratched the surface. Surely others already have emerged, or will in the future, to augment my report.

In 1915, the Turks drove the majority of the people of Armenia out into the wastes of the desert. Hundreds of thousands of Armenians died of starvation, exhaustion, and

R' Shlomo Zalman Auerbach

sunstroke in the desert. Experts estimate that more than a million additional Armenians perished during World War I. However, this massacre was soon forgotten by the world. When Hitler's advisers cautioned him that the world would not stand idly by as the Jews were being annihilated, he replied, "Who still speaks today of the massacre of the Armenians?" The genocide against the Jews, he felt, would just as quickly be forgotten.

I hope that this publication will help to arouse among us awareness of the Holocaust and aid in the continued study of its implications. Public outrage and revulsion is the most potent weapon we possess to prevent its recurrence. The world must never be permitted to forget the evil that was done.

In the summer of 1992, my husband was privileged to visit the great Gaon, Harav Shlomo Zalman Auerbach *zt"l* at his home in Jerusalem. When he informed him of his book, "Lest We Forget," published by Artscroll/Mesorah, the Gaon appeared delighted to hear that yet another book on the Holocaust had been published.

However, he then commented that such books should always contain a brief overview of the reaction of the nations of the world in regard to this catastrophe. Did anyone really care?

In addition the Gaon suggested that a proper response be offered to the many accusations leveled at our *kedoshim* for their lack of physical resistance to the Nazi tyranny.

In compliance with the Gaon's suggestions, the two final chapters of this book deal exclusively with these matters.

 ACKNOWLEDGMENTS

TAKE THIS OPPORTUNITY TO EXPRESS MY DEEP feelings of gratitude and appreciation to several people who helped make this work a reality.

Throughout the years, Hagaon Harav Pinchas Hirschprung *zt"l* has constantly reminded me of my obligation to publish a volume relating my experiences during the dark days of the Holocaust. The Gaon himself had published such a book relating his own experiences under the Nazi regime. His ever-inspiring words certainly went a long way in motivating me to tell my story.

Our own daughter-in-law, Dr. Miryam Wahrman, the Co-Director of the Center for Holocaust and Genocide Studies at William Paterson University, rarely failed to remind me of my responsibilities in this area. When we witness so many contemporary anti-Semitic elements investing so much time and effort to deny the very existence of a Holocaust, when the destruction of European Jewry is touted as a Jewish myth foisted upon the world to wrest reparations from Germany, then eyewitness reports of survivors, now more than ever, are of utmost importance. Hagaon Harav Eliezer Silver *zt"l* and Hagaon Harav Moshe Feinstein *zt"l* had expressed similar sentiments to my husband more than 40 years ago.

It is an honor, indeed, to be associated with Harav Meir Zlotowitz and Harav Nosson Scherman of ArtScroll Publications. These are men of great distinction who, through their many literary publications, are constantly spreading the word of genuine Torah among the masses. Their Schottenstein Talmud has become the key which has unlocked the gates of Torah studies for untold thousands. They are perhaps the greatest disseminators of Hashem's Torah today. I hereby extend to them my most sincere thanks and gratitude for permitting me to join the ranks of Artscroll contributors. May Hashem grant that they continue in their valiant efforts to promote authentic Torah and *Yiddishkeit* for many more years to come.

Mrs. Peninah Mizrachi spent many hours of her own time typing the original manuscript. Mrs. Debra Wenger meticulously reviewed the entire manuscript and immensely enhanced its quality. Binyamin Alpert and Yehoshua Chaitowsky, both students at the Mestiva of Nassau County, graciously assisted with the computer work. I thank them all wholeheartedly.

Mrs. Devorah Schechter's efforts should receive special mention. Her talents have vastly augmented the book's value. Her penetrating questions and invaluable suggestions were always on target. As a true friend, she worked beyond the call of duty and her enthusiasm for this project greatly inspired me. For all of this, I am most grateful. R' Eli Kroen produced the moving cover and Danny Kay and Hindy Goldner worked on pagination and graphics. Mrs. Faigie Weinbaum and Mrs. Mindy Stern proofread the manuscript, and Rifky Bruck, Shaya Sonnenschein and Chumie Zaidman typeset the book.

I wish to express my most heartful thanks to my dear husband, Harav Shlomo Wahrman, without whose help and support this book could not have been written. As a Holocaust survivor, my husband is personally familiar with Nazi atrocities. His constant encouragement went a long way in motivating me to tell my story. In addition, his vast Torah knowledge certainly enriched the contents and enhanced the quality of this book.

May Hashem grant that we derive much "nachas" from our children, Yaakov Elimelech and Faygie, Yisrael Shmuel and Miryam, Chaim Dov and Breindy; from our grandchildren, Shavie Shaindel and Shlomo, Miriam Chanah and Avi, Sima Esther and Yehudah Zev, Yosef Yehudah Aryeh, Avigail Rivkah, Shoshanah Nechamah, Yaakov Avrohom Note, Freida Rivkah; and from our great grandchildren, Rivkah, Avigial, Allegria Yehudis and Devorah. May we merit that Torah forever remain a way of life for our family, in fulfillment of the *Navi's* prophecy: "My spirit which is upon you and My words that I have placed in your mouth will not be withdrawn from your mouth nor from the mouth of your offspring nor from the mouth of your offspring's offspring, said Hashem, from this moment and forever" — ‏"רוּחִי אֲשֶׁר עָלֶיךָ וּדְבָרַי אֲשֶׁר שַׂמְתִּי בְּפִיךָ לֹא יָמוּשׁוּ מִפִּיךָ וּמִפִּי זַרְעֲךָ וּמִפִּי זֶרַע זַרְעֲךָ אָמַר ה' מֵעַתָּה וְעַד עוֹלָם"‏ (*Yeshayahu* 59:21).

HOPE NEVER DIES

A Survivor's Tale

CHAPTER ONE
Czechoslovakia Before World War II

ZECHOSLOVAKIA, LAND OF THE CZECHS and the Slovaks, is situated in the center of Europe. The Czechs live in the western part of the country, in Bohemia and Moravia, and the Slovaks live in the east in Slovakia. Both groups are of Slavic origin.

The country has beautiful scenery, with rugged snow-capped mountains, rounded hills, and rolling plains. Its natural resources include black, fertile farmlands and valuable minerals. This landlocked country is completely surrounded by other countries. It has always depended on some other countries for protection. The area belonged to Austria-Hungary before World War I. In the period between the two world wars, Czechoslovakia was a free republic. After World War II,

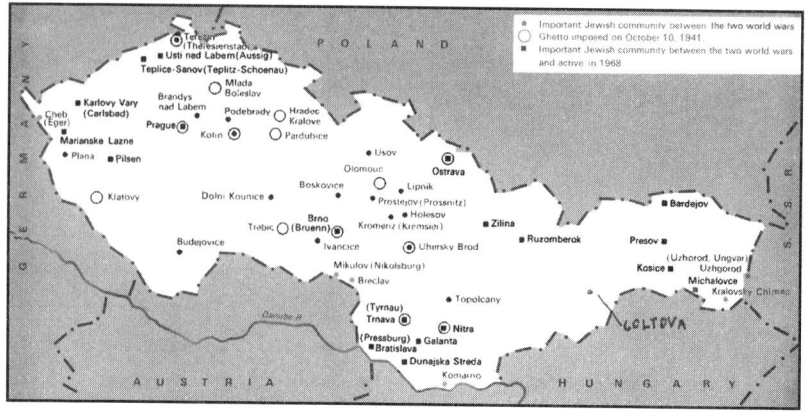

Map of Czechoslovakia

it became a Communist police state. Only recently has the country been divided. The Czech Republic is now situated in the west and Slovakia in the east.

When the Hapsburg government of Austria-Hungary entered World War I, the government took severe action against revolutionary movements in Bohemia. The leader of the Czech nationalists at the time was Tomas G. Masaryk. He and his young assistant, Edward Benes, fled to Switzerland and eventually moved to Paris. Their ultimate plan was to win the support of the Allies and create an independent Slavic state.

Thousands of Czech and Slovak soldiers surrendered to Russian and Italian forces. The Czechs and Slovaks in France, Russia, and the United States organized military units to fight with the Allies. Masaryk and Benes formed a Czechoslovak National Committee. They finally met in the United States and signed the Pittsburgh agreement, which provided that Czechs and Slovaks would unite equally in the new country. The Allies recognized the provisional government as the government of the Czechoslovak peoples.

In 1918, the Hapsburg government began to crumble, and Czechoslovakia declared itself an independent republic. Masaryk became the first president of the new country and Benes guided its foreign relations.

ANTI-SEMITISM AMONG ALL THE NATIONALITIES OF the republic was longstanding. When the republic was

Anti-Semitism in Czechoslovakia

established, there were anti-Semitic riots in Prague and in Holesov (Moravia). In Slovakia, serious anti-Semitic violence continued until the summer of 1919. Among the Czech elements it was less noticeable, mainly because of the personal example of Thomas Masaryk and Edward Benes and the democratic philosophy as expounded by them and the head of the Czechoslovak church, Hromadka.

However, many right-wing groups explicitly supported anti-Semitism in their platforms. Sudetenland, where many Germans resided, was already a stronghold of anti-Semitism under the Hapsburg monarchy. Anti-Semitism grew even more violent, influenced by the rise of Nazism in Germany, with the advent of Hitler to power.

Anti-Semitism in Czechoslovakia was strongly associated with the general conflicts among the nationalities there. The Czechs could not forgive the adherence of many Jews to the German language and culture and their support of the German liberal parties. In Slovakia and Carpatho-Russia, the Jews were considered the bearers of Magyarization and later supporters of the Czech establishment. Many alleged that the Jews were supporters of Communism.

After Hitler's rise to power, his growing support for German extreme nationalist demands and the enmity he manifested toward the Czech establishment drew the Jews increasingly closer to the Czech state, which all Jewish groups supported in its stand against Nazism. Post-World War I Czechoslovakia, which was relatively progressive and stable, was a congenial milieu for Czechoslovakian Jewry. Hence, most of them failed to see the dangers threatening them, even inside the country.

The subdued popular anti-Semitism was soon rekindled in Czechoslovakia. It gained strength in early 1938, when the Goga government came to power in Romania, and many Jewish refugees attempted to enter Czechoslovakia. Ferdinand Peroutka, the editor of a respected liberal weekly, published a series of articles calling for a restriction of Jewish rights. The problem of Jewish refugees became even more acute when Nazi Germany occupied Austria and many refugees, some holding Czechoslovakian passports, entered the country. Manifestations of anti-Semitism in Slovakia and the Sudeten area greatly increased.

At the time of the Munich conference (September 29, 1938), when the Sudetenland was handed over to the Germans on a silver platter by the leaders of France, Great Britain, and Italy, more than 20,000 Jews fled to the remaining territory of the state. Parts of Slovakia and Carpatho-Russia, with a Jewish population of approximately 80,000, were ceded to Hungary by decree of Hitler and Mussolini on November 2, 1938. Thus, Hungary occupied a large slice of land in southern Slovakia and Poland took 400 square miles of Czech territory near the city of Ostrava. Anti-Semitism rapidly became increasingly violent in Slovakia as well. On March 14, 1939, Slovakia declared its independence and became a vassal of Nazi Germany. The next day, the remaining parts of Bohemia and Moravia were occupied by the Germans and transformed into a German protectorate.

CHAPTER 2
GROWING UP IN
A TIME OF UPHEAVAL

IT WAS IN CZECHOSLOVAKIA, DURING THESE troubled times, that I spent my early years. I was born in the village of Ilnica, which is located in the Carpatho-Russia region of the country. Since my family left Ilnica before I even reached my first birthday, I know very little about my birthplace; it remains merely a geographic location, without any special significance.

Following our departure from Ilnica, the family's sojourns then took us for brief periods to Orechova, to Gicce, and eventually to Coltova, which is located in the vicinity of Tornalya. It was there in Coltova that I spent my early years.

Life in Coltova abruptly ended in 1944, however, when all Jews were deported by the Hungarian Nazis.

HaRav Yoel Teitelbaum, the Satmar Rav

When we resided in Orechova, the community's chief rabbi was the young Rav Yoel Teitelbaum. He eventually became the chief rabbi of the large Satmar community in Romania. Yet, even in his pre-Satmar days, he had already established his credentials and was a renowned Torah figure on the Jewish scene. His outstanding scholarship, combined with his great piety, had already spread his reputation far and wide. His opinions and rulings in Jewish law were widely accepted.

During our few short years in Orechova, my father was always in close contact with Rav Teitelbaum. He rarely missed a *shiur* (Torah lecture) taught by the Rav. He felt a great reverence for the man who possessed such eminent qualifications. He considered Rav Teitelbaum not only to be a Torah giant, but also a *tzaddik*, a man of the highest caliber, and he admired him intensely. His devotion toward him was unquestionable.

This feeling appeared to be mutual indeed. When my husband visited the Satmar Rebbe in his residence in Brooklyn in 1956 and informed him of his relationship to my father, the Rebbe immediately responded, "Ah, Reb Yaakov Elimelech — he was one of my students." He then added rather sadly, "Where can we find such Jews nowadays? Reb Yaakov Elimelech was truly a genuine *tzaddik.*" He concluded, "*Hashem yinkom es damo* — May Hashem avenge his blood."

My brother, Shlomo Zalmen, was born during our brief stay in Orechova, and the family was overjoyed when Rav Teitelbaum consented to be the *sandek* at his *bris*. It was truly a great honor he had bestowed on our appreciative family.

When Rav Teitelbaum eventually left Orechova to become the chief rabbi of Satmar, it was quite a blow to the community. The city had been accustomed to being guided by great *gedolim*. Prior to Rav Teitelbaum, Rav Levi Yitzchok Greenwald, known as the Tzelemer Rav, was the city's spiritual leader. He later moved to the Williamsburg section of Brooklyn, where he founded the Tzelemer *kehillah* and the Yeshiva and Mesivta Arugas Habosem. My father was a *shochet,* a ritual slaughterer, who had received his *Kabbalah,* permitting him to slaughter, fron the Tzelemer Rav.

It is no wonder, therefore, that Orechova's butcher shop, which was run by my father, flourished beyond all expectations. Even communities quite distant from Orechova chose to purchase the meat whose *kashrus* was approved and recommended by such a trustworthy *tzaddik as* Harav Teitelbaum. Since he was the *Rav Hamachshir,* people reasoned, there could no longer be the slightest doubt as to the meat's *kashrus*. Unfortunately, as a result of the Rav's departure, the butcher shop began a steep downward trend, from which it never recovered. It faltered and went out of existence. My family then moved to Gicce, and a short time thereafter, we settled in Coltova.

I was the second of eight children born to my parents, Yaakov Elimelech and Frieda Herskovits. There were four boys and four girls. As I mentioned, my father earned his livelihood as a *shochet*. It was a life of arduous labor, as he generally performed his services not just for his own community members, but also for neighboring villages who had no *shochet* of their own. A bicycle was his means of transportation. This created tremendous hardships for him, especially during the extreme Czechoslovakian winter, when temperatures hover near and below zero degrees Fahrenheit. In addition, bicycles are certainly not adequate conveyers over icy and snow-covered roads.

My father had a most difficult time merely earning a living for such a large family, and thus we survived on the bare

My family at Coltova in 1939. My parents and the three youngest children did not survive.

essentials of life. Splendor, extravagance, and excess never entered our home. However, as youngsters, we were never aware of our financial woes. Our family was very close knit. There was a natural feeling of love among us all. We were content with our own lot in life. As far as we were concerned, we were rich. We possessed everything we ever needed. As our sages taught us in *Pirkei Avos*: "Who is a wealthy person? One who is happy with his lot" — "אֵיזֶהוּ עָשִׁיר הַשָּׂמֵחַ בְּחֶלְקוֹ".

There was, however, one negative feature we unfortunately had to endure in our life in Coltova. Due to its tiny Jewish population, it was virtually impossible to assemble a *minyan* for the purpose of conducting public religious services throughout the week. Only on Shabbos and Yom Tov were such services possible. Throughout the week we, in fact, resided in a village practically devoid of any meaningful Jewish life. This troubled my parents greatly. It was difficult to raise children to value a life of Torah in such spiritually barren surroundings. My father continually searched for a position in a city more imbued with a Torah atmosphere, but his efforts did not meet with success.

There had been an offer of a position in the city of Roznava, the largest town in our area. Its population approached 10,000 and it boasted a substantial Jewish *kehillah*. However many of its Jewish residents were of the Neologist persuasion — Neology was the unofficial name of the communities in Hungary belonging to the Reform movement. If my father had accepted the position as a *shochet* in Roznava, he would have been able to perform his duties in one town, rather than in the 18 scattered villages that he visited periodically as part of his position in Coltova. What an easy life this could have been! His economic resources would have risen dramatically and he could have raised his family in tranquil surroundings, while living among Jews.

However, my father respectfully declined the offer. He was greatly concerned about the effect Neologists would have on his young children. Perhaps they would succeed in implanting their own philosophy within them and thus, inculcate in them ways totally foreign to the Torah. For my father, Torah education of his children far outweighed any economic considerations. It was the essence of his existence and he was fortunate, indeed, to have as his life's partner a woman who was as dedicated to the same principles as my mother was. She was a genuine *aishes chayil* in the fullest sense of the word. Naturally, she shared my father's values and was greatly relieved by my father's decision to remain in Coltova.

Thus, while residing in Coltova, my father's bicycle took him to 18 neighboring villages to perform his services as a *shochet*. Twice weekly, he left home in the predawn hours and returned home late at night. These were indeed strenuous days for him and he usually returned home physically exhausted.

His expert knowledge of the working mechanics of clocks and watches enabled him to supplement his *shechitah* income. During a large part of the week, he repaired clocks and watches for the good citizens of Coltova. When he repaired the clocks

Area around Coltava

of local farmers he was paid with fresh fruits, vegetables, eggs, and sometimes even with live chickens, rather than with cash. This went a long way towards feeding a family of 10.

Since they were residents of such a tiny village, Coltovians were certainly not able to afford the services of their own rabbi. Fortunately, however, my father was able to fill this vacuum with flying colors, and all spiritual leadership was thrust upon his shoulders. Our *shul* was a magnificent structure, constructed jointly by Jews of seven local villages. It was located right next to our own home and was actually attached to it. One had to ascend a flight of 10 steps in order to reach a large anteroom which eventually led to the synagogue's portals.

My father's duties involved the conducting of services. He was the permanent *ba'al tefillah*, its *ba'al korei*, and its *ba'al toke'a* for the High Holidays. He performed many other synagogue functions as well. He responded to many *halachic* questions addressed to him. Being a genuine Torah scholar, he was adequately qualified to perform such rabbinical activities. My father, a most pious individual, was a well-liked and admired figure in his community. People treated him with the utmost

A typical street in Coltova

reverence, generally trusted his *halachic* decisions and judgments, and relied on them. When, however, a more difficult *sha'alah* reached my father's desk, one that required extensive rabbinical knowledge and involvement, he generally referred the questioner to Harav Ephraim Balaita, who was the official *dayan* in the town of Tornalya.

FOR A PERIOD OF EIGHT YEARS, I ATTENDED THE LOCAL school in Coltova. The first semester of the first school year

My Education — Both in School and out

turned out to be a disaster for me, as I had great difficulties mastering the art of reading. As a result, I presented my parents with a failing report card, feeling inferior and emotionally overcome. I expected to be chastised by my parents. I felt that I had let them down. They deserved better from me. However, rather than displaying any feeling of disappointment and frustration, my parents uttered not a single word of criticism. They remained calm and serene. It was then that my father's warm and affectionate personality made itself very apparent. His kindness overwhelmed me as he gently placed me on his knees, took my book, and began to

Our neighbor's house in Coltova

read with me. Together we read and we read. This eventually became a daily session and gradually, my reading ability began to improve. I had loved hearing stories and the book opened my eyes to a wonderful world of stories. I learned quickly, and by the end of the year I was the best reader in the class.

My father was able to handle matters with the utmost kindness. With a smile and a hug, he always knew the right words to cheer up people, even those in a state of great emotional distress. His warm and cheerful personality could melt even the iciest hearts. His *gemilus chassadim*, his lovingkindness, had no match.

Once, when I was eight years old, I saw a bird on the ground, attempting to fly. But, alas, it was too young and it was unable to do so satisfactorily. I picked it up and brought it home. I was overjoyed to have my own bird. I had always wanted a bird for a pet.

My father gently inquired as to how I planned to feed it. It was a wild bird and ate nothing but insects. I promised to catch insects and feed them to the bird. "This bird is too young," my father retorted, "and it does not yet know how to eat by itself."

He then explained how the mother bird feeds its young. It assembles insects in its own beak and then places them into the baby bird's beak. "Could you do that?" he asked.

Since my father was firmly convinced that the baby bird had fallen from its nest, he felt that its mother was surely looking for it. He therefore suggested that we place it on top of the well we had in our yard, which was covered by a concrete top, and watch it. In the eventuality that the mother bird would not come to retrieve it within a short time, my father promised to help me raise it; otherwise, he said, I should permit the mother to take back its young.

Reluctantly, I handed the bird to my father, who ever so gently placed it on top of the well. Sure enough, the young bird's chirping attracted its mother, and I sadly watched both slowly disappear from sight. With tears rolling down my cheeks, I hastened to my father who embraced me lovingly. He exerted every effort to comfort me and to console me for my loss. He then informed me of the great *mitzvah* I had just performed. To return a baby to its mother is certainly a righteous deed. "Hashem will surely reward you for your act of kindness," he promised.

I shall always remember another incident of my childhood which again evidenced my father's total dedication to a life of *chesed*. To assist others with warmth and genuine love, was, indeed, the motto and guiding principle of his life. Our family raised poultry; chickens, turkeys, and geese. Since I had always wanted a pet of my own, I pretended that these were actually my pets. I simply loved feeding them and always made sure that they didn't go hungry. My favorite pastime was to take a piece of bread and sit down on the lawn. It was wonderful when the geese surrounded me to receive their crumbs! They were so attached to me that they came running to me whenever I left the house.

Once someone accidentally stepped on a baby goose and it was injured. How sad I felt! I was extremely downcast. I gently picked it up, and with tears in my eyes, I brought it to my father. After a thorough examination, my father diagnosed the injury as merely a broken wing. He placed the wing in a sling and assured me that the goose would probably survive, although it would remain crippled for life. He permitted me to bring the goose into the kitchen, where I constructed a nest for it. Slowly, I was able to nurse it back to health.

My father's conjecture proved to be correct. The goose did recover substantially. However, its broken wing was never again firmly attached so it hung down. As a result, it could never fly again. The goose eventually became my unsolicited companion. It followed me wherever I went. It rarely joined the other geese. It even escorted me to school, and while I was inside the building it patiently waited outside, honking from time to time. How happy it appeared as we left the school together!

My mother too, was a living role model for *gemilas chassadim*. When hungry strangers arrived at our home, she would always welcome them with open arms. They were generally treated as honored guests and felt right at home in our modest and humble abode. Often, when food supplies were scarce, my mother would contribute her own supper meal to still the hunger of the strangers. As a result, our home became a popular address for many poverty-stricken unfortunates in Coltova and its surroundings.

I can still vividly recall one specific Friday morning, perhaps in 1936. It was in the midst of the winter season, when the daylight hours were extremely short. My mother rose at 4 a.m. to prepare the Shabbos meals for a family of 10. Approximately at 11 a.m. four hungry Chassidic Jews from other communities arrived at our door and my mother graciously offered them coffee and the freshly baked cakes. They ate to their hearts' content.

Soon, my mother discovered that these hungry guests had consumed the entire supply of cake. Although greatly saddened and downcast by the fact that our own family would now be deprived of this delicious delicacy for this particular Shabbos, the guests never detected her state of dejection. She eventually escorted them to the door, thanked them for their visit, and urged them to come again. I certainly learned a valuable lesson about the *mitzvah* of *hachnasas orchim* on that Friday.

Near the end of my eighth school year, my teacher inquired about my plans after graduation: Was I considering continuing my education by attending a school of higher learning? With tears in my eyes, I responded that since my parents firmly believed that my future did not lie in the schools, my formal education would be terminated at the end of that school year.

The teacher, however, was too highly devoted to his students to permit this matter to stand unchallenged. He was quite persistent, and decided to visit our home to persuade my parents to attempt to change their apparently negative attitude toward advanced education. He did succeed to a certain degree, as he was able to convince my parents that it would be a waste of my talents for me to drop out of school and not avail myself of the opportunity to pursue higher education. Despite my shortcomings in the field of mathematics, the teacher felt that I was an exceptional student who possessed excellent capabilities, with a memory second to none. My own personal feelings were quite clear: I truly loved school and it was breaking my heart that I would soon have to drop out.

Suddenly, however, there appeared a silver lining amidst the clouds. I overheard my parents discussing my future in light of the teacher's visit and they decided, unexpectedly, to help me become a schoolteacher. I was delighted! My education would, after all, not be terminated at the end of the school year.

Although my ambition had always been to pursue a career in the practice of medicine, I had never expressed these aspirations to my parents. Let me accomplish one thing at a time, I felt. Let me first enter the field of higher education. Then I would gradually begin to focus on the medical field.

UNFORTUNATELY, BEFORE MY FATHER EVEN HAD THE opportunity to register me in the gymnasium, all my dreams

Shattered Dreams were shattered. Hungary occupied a section of Czechoslovakia, and things were never the same again. I can still remember the Hungarian soldiers marching into town, singing the most horrendous anti-Semitic songs.

From that day on, persecution of the Jews increased daily. The barbaric and cruel behavior of the Hungarians knew no bounds. It was a free-for-all against the entire Jewish population.

The Hungarians abruptly decreed that henceforth, higher education for Jews was strictly forbidden. That decree, for all practical purposes, shattered all my dreams in the area of education. Suddenly a powerful feeling penetrated my mind. I realized that I *was* different, that I *am* different, and that the secular world was reserving special treatment for me and for all other Jews. We were *all* different. At the time, I could not yet realize the full extent of this special treatment. Did anyone anticipate gas chambers and concentration camps in our future? For me personally, however, the entry of the Hungarian army into Coltova marked the beginning of the Holocaust. It was the beginning of the end for me.

Since Bais Yaakov schools did not exist in Hungary and Czechoslovakia, our Torah education took place solely in the home. Fortunately, our parents were totally dedicated to a Torah way of life and, as a result, were highly successful in transmitting the words of Hashem to each one of us. We were taught well. Eventually, my parents hired a private tutor. Besides receiving free room and board at our home, this tutor, Reb Shimon, received a weekly salary. He faithfully complied with all responsibilities thrust upon him, and thus, made a giant contribution to our spiritual growth.

Two of my brothers, Shlomo Zalmen and Chaim Leib, attended the yeshiva in Balassagyarmat in northern Hungary, not far from the Slovakian border. They entered the yeshiva in their pre-*bar mitzvah* years. Their *bar mitzvahs* were then celebrated at the yeshiva, without the extravagance and splendor that are so prevalent in American *bar mitzvah* celebrations today. Chaim Leib shed bitter tears on his *bar mitzvah* day, for he felt desolate and homesick, longing for his home and his family. However, he never expressed any qualms about attending the yeshiva, for he was fully convinced that the yeshiva was the only means available for him to become a genuine *talmid chacham* and a Torah-true Jew.

When I first began to realize that I would never again go to school, I suddenly lost my voice. I was only able to whisper. My parents, naturally, were greatly concerned about my condition and when it persisted, with no apparent improvement, they consulted a doctor who recommended further tests in the hospital in Roznava, the largest town in the region. All test results were negative, but my voice did not return for six months. It was felt that my problem was emotional in nature, in the main brought about by my exclusion from the school system. Of course, everyone was delighted when my voice returned, but my anxieties and irritations remained intact. I despised the Hungarians, the new rulers of the country, for their anti-Semitic policies, which closed all doors to my further education.

My father, recognizing my depressed frame of mind, searched vigorously for means to placate my troubled mind and succeeded in discovering a viable solution to my problems. Familiar with my love and affection for animals, he bought five angora rabbits for me . They were beautiful animals with long white hair and red eyes. He built cages for them, and it became my responsibility to take care of them. How I loved my work!

Since rabbits multiply rapidly and produce six to eight offspring each month, we had as many as 55 rabbits the following year. I derived so much pleasure from my work that my exclusion from school was no longer a problem. I had adjusted beautifully to my new duties.

MEANWHILE, DRASTIC CHANGES TOOK PLACE IN OUR country, which had become part of the Hungarian nation. In

The Situation Becomes More Grave conformity with the Third Jewish Law (1941), which defined the term "Jew" in more radical terms, 58,320 persons previously not belonging to the Jewish faith were now considered Jewish. Thus, the total number of persons officially registered as Jews in mid-1941 was more than 803,000. These were people liable to racial discrimination.

The Third Jewish Law, based on the infamous Nuremberg laws of Nazi Germany, strictly prohibited intermarriage. By mid-1941, the anti-Jewish measures had placed Hungarian Jewry in a most disadvantageous position in every sphere of political, economic, cultural, and social life. The government party Magyar Elet Partja (MEP, or the Party of Hungarian Life) pursued a pro-Nazi anti-Semitic policy, while various national-socialist groupings exerted increasing pressure on the government to stiffen its anti-Jewish policy.

The decimation of the Jewish population began in the autumn of 1940, shortly after the incorporation of northern Transylvania. Thousands of Jews whose citizenship was in question were forcibly expelled from there mainly to Romania.

The first large-scale loss of life among Hungarian Jewry occurred in July 1941, when the Office for Alien Control expelled about 20,000 Jews, whose Hungarian citizenship was in doubt, to German-held Galicia. Most of these people were inhabitants of the areas annexed from Czechoslovakia. They were mostly concentrated in the Kamenets-Podolsk area.

The Germans demanded that these Jews be sent back, as they could not cope with them. The Hungarian government refused. A senior SS officer, Lieutenant-General Franz Jaeckeln, then assured the conference of the German military authorities held in Vinnitsa that he would complete the liquidation of those Jews by September 1941.

Between August 27 and August 29, the Jews were marched out of Kamenets-Podolsk to a series of bomb craters 10 miles outside the town. There, they were ordered to undress and they were machine-gunned. Many were buried alive. Franz Jaeckeln had kept his promise.

Leslie Gordon, one of the survivors of the massacre, vividly described the scene. "The naked Jews were then sent to the ditches while SS men, some of them drunk and some of them photographing the scene, completed their task. All in the ditches were executed. Many were only hurt, but were buried alive.

"After the shooting, as we were ordered to throw some earth on the bodies, some were still crying for help. Eventually, several trucks with quick-lime arrived and were emptied upon the earth. All in all, the entire scene resembled a slaughter-house. How low had humans sunk!"

ONE OF THE NEW MEASURES INSTITUTED BY THE Hungarian Nazis, which greatly affected the economic future

A New Vocation

of our own family, was the prohibition of *shechitah*. My father, who earned his livelihood in this profession, no longer had any means to support his family. What a devastating experience for a man who had to sustain a family of 10! How could we survive under these conditions?

Despite the ban on *shechitah*, our family continued to eat chicken at regular intervals. Since we owned much poultry in Coltova, my father performed the act of *shechitah* for our immediate family in a secret, surreptitious manner. Occasionally, close neighbors would bring poultry to our home for the purpose of *shechitah*. But this was only on a small scale, only for several individuals. For all practical purposes, my father was unemployed.

The family, therefore, embarked on a new business venture. My father dispatched me to a neighboring town, where I learned the art of shearing rabbit's fur and then weaving it into yarn. My father purchased a spinning wheel and with intensive practice, I was able to master the art of spinning the angora yarn. Since we owned many rabbits at the time, there was certainly no shortage of yarn. We were now open for business.

My younger sister Golde was (and still is) a knitter *par excellence*. Knitting the yarn became her responsibility, while my older sister Fayge, who was an expert and established seamstress, made sweaters, hats, and many other items from the knitted yarn. Everyone pitched in to produce merchandise.

It was not difficult at all to publicize our business. Coltovians and people from other towns were generally aware of the beautiful clothes available in our house, and they came in droves to purchase them. A clothing store in Tornalya constantly promoted our goods and supplies rarely were able to keep up with demands. With the help of Hashem, our once-desperate financial situation ceased to be a disaster.

Although I personally even performed spinning work for other people who possessed angora farms, my parents refused to accept any money I earned from these outside services. It was my money, they insisted. However, with a major war in progress and vast shortages existing in many areas, I could not find a better place to invest my money than in spending it on my loving family. So I purchased quantities of scarce food items which, at times, consisted of sacks of grains and bushels of fruit. This kept us going for a while, at least.

CHAPTER 3
LEAVING HOME

ITH THE RAPID INCREASE OF PERSECUTIONS and oppression of the Jews throughout Hungary, it was inevitable that the long and treacherous arm of Hitler's Nazis would eventually reach us. The specter constantly grew darker. Suddenly, the Nazi machine arrived within our midst, supported by its full military power. Our family was now personally involved, as two of my mother's brothers, my uncle Yaakov and my uncle Yisroel, were unexpectedly snatched from their homes and dispatched to forced labor camps. "We need every able-bodied man to intensify and enhance the war effort," the government claimed.

At the same time, my uncle's wives and their children, totaling eight precious youngsters, and my 72-year-old maternal grandfather were transported to Kamenets-Podolsk, where

My grandparents, Aharon and Esther Hershkovitz

they were forced to dig their own graves (while being convinced that they were actually digging antitank ditches to retard the Russian army's steady advance) and then were shot by the SS.

My grandfather apparently had been scheduled for a later shooting. As a result, he was merely a spectator when so many of his family members were so brutally liquidated. Just imagine the emotions which erupted within this 72-year-old man as he stood there helpless, unable to come to the rescue! Just imagine the torment and agony he suffered! The cruelty inflicted on him is beyond human comprehension!

Among those who witnessed this massacre was a young girl named Surie Weiss, who, after the war, would marry my brother, Chaim Leib. She and her family of seven, along with an additional Hungarian family, had been brought to the area apparently to also become victims of the massacre. When they realized that their own turn would soon be at hand, my grandfather and those two other families instinctively began to flee as fast as their feet would carry them. Why the SS made no serious attempt to pursue the escapees remains an enigma to me.

Tornalya today

They were able to hide in a nearby forest to recoup their energies. Eventually, they commenced a journey on foot to their homes, a journey that lasted more then four weeks. Begging from families along the way was their sole means of subsistence, and the outdoors became their sleeping quarters.

At one point, they met what appeared to be a kindhearted German, who directed them to a nearby village, which was the residence of several Jewish families. These Jews were very helpful to the wandering escapees and generously offered them food and lodging.

Suddenly, the supposedly kindhearted German appeared, and fatally shot a Hungarian Jew. Surie's father was then ordered to bury him. My grandfather was saved from this massacre, as he was in the lavatory at the time.

After a long and arduous journey, my grandfather returned to his home in Solywa, Hungary. There he was arrested by the authorities because of his unscheduled return. From his jail cell he was able to write to us, informing us of the sad events. We would never see him again. Most likely, he perished together with his fellow Jews in a Nazi concentration camp.

One day, in 1941, the mayor of Tornalya, escorted by two policemen, arrived at our home. Since we had never met the mayor before, we had no idea who this man was. Yet, at the sight of the two policemen, we all froze with fright. We were in a state of utmost terror. What was the purpose of their abrupt visit? What did they want from us? Had they come to arrest us? When the mayor noticed our alarm and panic, he quickly apologized and immediately began to pacify us. He had not come in the capacity of a town official, but, rather, as an ordinary private citizen.

He then pointed to me, sitting at my spinning wheel, and informed us that he was looking for me. "But she is so young," he added. I suggested to him that he not judge me by my appearance, since I was older than I looked. He then explained that he owned an angora farm and since the reputation of my outstanding spinning ability had spread far and wide, he would like me to work for him. I accepted the job. It was really a pleasure working for him, as he was a true gentleman and he paid me well. It was not, however, a steady job, as every so often, the mayor's farm did not have a sufficient supply of wool for me to spin.

It was during this period of my life that, from time to time, I would travel to the city of Sanpeter, in the vicinity of Debrecin. I was always a most welcome guest at the home of the rabbi of Sanpeter and I usually would remain there for approximately a week. The rabbi resided there with his wife and when his son-in-law was taken to forced labor, his daughter and granddaughter moved in. To enable his daughter to earn a livelihood, the rabbi purchased an angora farm for her and it became my task to shear the rabbits and spin the yarn.

The rabbi's daughter, Marishka, and I developed a close friendship. There was a mutual feeling of love between us. She was always kind to me. She was older than I was and treated me with all the love of a mother. She showered me with attention and never ceased offering me compliments. She was a true friend and helped me build a positive self-image. I could have been so happy, if only the times weren't so perilous. However, we lived in a state of fear and apprehension often bordering on hysteria, as the Nazi persecution continued relentlessly.

Because of quota regulations, Jews were slowly eased out of the professions, commerce, journalism, schools, universities, and public employment. Jewish participation in various fields was not to exceed certain percentages fixed by law: for example, 6 percent in trade, 6 percent in the professions, and 12 percent of the labor force in individual firms.

By the end of 1942, Jews had been ousted completely from certain fields and more than 200,000 Jews had lost their customary work. This created severe hardships for the Jewish masses and, in some cases, there were last-ditch efforts to join allowable trades. However, there were too many applicants for the available jobs. The Hungarian government closed this gap by resorting to forced-labor projects. The basis of the forced-labor system was a law under which Jews were liable for "auxiliary service" in the Hungarian army, as distinguished from armed service. Soon thereafter, Hungary declared war against Russia. Jews were conscripted into labor units and were exposed to fearful atrocities.

These labor units were sent to the Russian front together with regular army troops. Their numbers reached 50,000. After the great breakthrough of the advancing Soviet army near the river Don, the Hungarian army disintegrated and its soldiers fled in panic. It is estimated that more than 40,000 of the original 50,000 Jews died during the retreat, many from hunger, typhus, and outright murder.

Jews in the Hungarian labor units worked with army engineers building roads and bridges and clearing mines under penal conditions, often as inhuman as those in the German concentration camps. When the war broke out, tens of thousands of conscripts, insufficiently clothed, were sent to frontier districts occupied by the Hungarian troops. Most of these early contingents perished. Among those who perished was our physician, Dr. Balasa from Plesivec. Hangings, shootings, and cruel beatings were commonplace. There was absolutely no regard for Jewish life.

Sometimes there were mass killings, as in the military hospital near Korasten, where 500 conscripts lay ill with typhoid fever. One night, the hospital was ringed with machine guns and set on fire. Those who attempted to flee were shot down.

There were reports of so-called shooting parties, in which Jews would be forced to climb trees and, like monkeys, jump from branch to branch. If they fell, they were pierced with bayonets; if they jumped too slowly, they were driven by guards wielding whips and sticks. Sometimes they were suspended from the trees by their tied wrists. If they fainted, they would be drenched with cold water and left to freeze in the Russian cold. Other conscripts were chained and thrown into campfires.

WITH SUCH PREVAILING CONDITIONS, MY FATHER made every effort to extricate us from this Hungarian jungle.

Our Attempts to Escape the War Machine He left no corner unexplored. His first target was Palestine. He made a firm decision to apply to the British consulate for a certificate that would enable us to immigrate to *Eretz Yisrael*. He felt that Palestine would be the safest haven for us. After all, this was *Eretz Yisrael*, our very own homeland.

In preparation for our possible immigration to Palestine, my father purchased a small tract of land in Coltova, where we learned how to grow vegetables and grain. Agriculture might be the only means to sustain ourselves in Palestine, my father reasoned. Everyone was put to work. All of the older children worked in the fields. Even my mother, who spent the bulk of her time doing household chores for a family of 10 and caring for the family's infants, participated actively in our family's agricultural endeavors. I was the only one excused from the fields, since my work in our angora farm was vital to our existence.

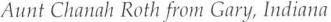

Aunt Chanah Roth from Gary, Indiana   *Uncle Chaim Ber Roth from Gary, Indiana*

However, we soon discovered that our aspirations to immigrate to Palestine would not be realized. With the advent of the Hitler years, the number of applications for certificates had grown tremendously and the British would issue only a small number of certificates each month. It would take years before our turn would come. Sadly, my parents conceded that we must search for another country that would accept us. Most countries had, unfortunately, locked their gates to Jewish immigration.

We pursued possibilities in other countries. We applied for immigration permits to the African countries of Ethiopia and to the French-controlled island of Madagascar (now the Malagasy Republic). Both countries had intimated their willingness to accept a small number of Jewish refugees. None of these opportunities bore fruit. The publicly announced quota numbers had already surpassed their limits.

My parents had also appealed to my mother's sister, Aunt Chanah Roth, and her husband, Uncle Chaim Ber, who resided in the United States in the city of Gary, Indiana. We explained the tragic situation confronting the Jews of Hungary and why it was imperative for us to emigrate from that *Gehennom*. Our lives were at stake here, we emphasized in our missive.

My aunt's reply came quickly. U.S. law required that a sponsor for new immigrants would have to submit an affidavit declaring that, under no circumstances, would the new immigrants ever become a burden to the United States. The sponsor would have to guarantee full financial support for the new immigrants, should they be unable to earn a livelihood.

Aunt Chanah was informed by authorities that her low income certainly would not be sufficient to support a family of 10, and thus her affidavit would be worthless. She then consulted an attorney, who advised her to attempt to bring us to the United States one by one.

An affidavit was first sent to my older sister Fayge and after a long delay, she finally received her immigration papers. She was now eligible to enter the United States. Her papers arrived several days before we were dragged to the ghetto. Once in the ghetto, her papers would become obsolete, as no one emigrated from there.

I remember quite clearly how my father begged and appealed to my sister Fayge to go to Aunt Chanah in America, but his pleas fell on deaf ears. My sister remained adamant and inflexible. "How can I go to the safety of America while my family is existing in such dire and dismal circumstances? How can I survive spiritually in the freedom of America, not knowing the whereabouts and the physical condition of my loved ones?"

By then, we all knew that our situation was hopeless. We lived under no illusions and we were aware of the fact that our situation would only slide further downhill. We knew that major persecutions and atrocities awaited us in the future. No one, however, could have foretold the severity of the Nazi actions.

My father was so concerned with our potential perilous future that he spent many sleepless nights. Often, during the night, he would get out of bed and head for the *shul*, where he recited chapters from the book of *Tehillim*. I could hear him through the open window and listened intently. He prayed in a melodious tone which reflected his mood, his passions, and inner emotions. He prayed with so much feeling and with so much *kavanah*, that I was able to feel the tears in his voice. He was pleading for his family and he was pleading for his people.

CHAPTER 4
THE NAZIS ARRIVE

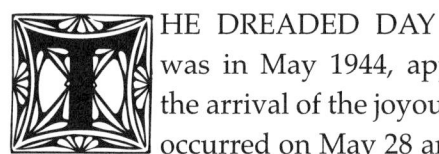HE DREADED DAY EVENTUALLY CAME. IT was in May 1944, approximately 10 days before the arrival of the joyous holiday of Shavuos, which occurred on May 28 and 29 of that particular year. Early in the morning, Hungarian policemen arrived at our home and informed us that on that morning we would be moved to the ghetto in the neighboring city of Tornalya. They suggested that we take along some food items and extra clothing because the duration of our stay was as yet undetermined. We packed up such essentials as bread, potatoes, onions, noodles, eggs, and also brought along some articles of clothing. We were on our way to what turned out to be a year of indescribable torture and torment, yet uncharted in the annals of human history.

It was quite obvious to us that the policemen were most reluctant to carry out their assignment. They insisted that they were keenly sorry and heartbroken by the subhuman treatment

The police station in Tornalya where we received physical examinations

accorded to us. But they really had no choice in the matter, they said; they were merely following government orders. All the way to Tornalya, they expressed their most sincere apologies to us, over and over again.

When we arrived in Tornalya, we were taken to the local police station. We were asked to undress and a thorough search of our clothing and bodies ensued. Even our most private body parts were grossly violated. The aim of the search was to find valuables we may have been hiding on our bodies and clothes, valuables that they intended to confiscate. Throughout the ordeal, they constantly apprised us of the fact that anyone caught concealing valuables would be severely punished.

They found no valuables on us. Several weeks earlier, in anticipation of a possible deportation, we had hidden many items in our house in Coltova. They were securely stored in the attic, between the dome of the *shul* and one of its walls. Somehow, my mother's wedding ring, which she openly displayed on her finger, was not detected by the scrutinizing eyes of the Hungarian police. The only thing confiscated at the time were my father's legal papers, which he had brought along.

Back of Feher Lo Hotel in Tornalya – area of the ghetto

The Hungarian woman who examined me apologized for the humiliation and abuse she had thrust upon me. But of course, she was merely following orders. She had no choice in the matter. I tended to believe her, as she was nice and sounded sincere. An ardent anti-Semite would have had no reason to address a Jewish girl in such a kind, gentle, and respectful manner.

Upon completion of the examination, we were taken to a local *Feher Lo* (White Horse) hotel, which was surrounded by a metal fence, guarded by the police. We were assigned to a small room, which we were to share with another family. It is difficult to comprehend the crowded conditions that prevailed. We were a family of 10 and the other family had five additional individuals. Just imagine a throng of 15 people confined to such a small area.

Since the room was not furnished with any beds, we were forced to sleep on the floor. The crowded conditions almost made us feel as if we were sleeping on top of each other. For approximately three weeks, we were confined in the Tornalya slum.

During the day, we were permitted to walk outdoors but not farther than the guarded fence. Escape was virtually hopeless. Besides, where would we go? Which place in Hungary would offer safety and security for Jews? Where could we hide?

One day, I discovered some books in the hotel's basement. I began to read. While reading, I had the capacity to concentrate on the book's contents to such an extent that I was able to lock out and forget all of my problems and anxieties. It was as if I had escaped to a new world, a world far removed from the persecutions and tortures of planet Earth. While reading, I felt calm, tranquil, and at ease. It was a brief respite for my weary and exhausted nerves.

My mother was greatly annoyed that I spent so much of my time simply reading. "These are perilous and hazardous times for the Jews," she exhorted, "and we must utilize every moment of our time, *davening* to Hashem, entreating Him and imploring Him to have mercy on His people, and save us from the abyss, from the bottomless pit in which we now found ourselves. Plead with Him to send the *Mashiach* swiftly!" Rather than read books, my mother felt we should recite chapters from the book of *Tehillim*. "Hashem is our only hope," she contended.

My father fully agreed that intervention with Hashem was vital. Yet he interjected in a friendly manner that he understood me quite clearly. He would also turn to reading, he added, if that would help him lock out our problems, even if only briefly.

The holiday of Shavuos, which occurred on the 10th day of our confinement, turned out to be a most tragic one. Early in the morning we were informed that my father and my brother Shlomo Zalmen would be taken to slave labor that day. My father was ordered to shave off his beard immediately.

The scene that unfolded before my eyes as my father began to cut his beard is one I shall never forget. It will remain engraved in my memory forever. All of us stood around the room with tears rolling down our cheeks, as we watched our father sadly obey his orders. We all felt that our father was being both degraded and humiliated. How low have they sunk, I thought to myself. How could any human being be so cruel to bring abuse to a man so devout and so pious?

My father attempted to bring a smile to our faces via some humorous remarks. It didn't work. When he was completely clean shaven, he looked like an entirely different person. His beard had added dignity to his persona. Now, gone were his personality, his luster, and his splendor. With uncontrollable tears in our eyes and with sadness and sorrow in our heart, we escorted our father up to the hotel's fence. With him was my brother Shlomo Zalmen, who was also scheduled for deportation that day.

A most moving and emotional scene transpired during our farewell. We hugged, we embraced, we kissed, and I screamed in anguish and agony. Would we ever see each other again? Was this the time when our warm relationship would end?

My father, unexpectedly, returned to us later the same day. However, Shlomo Zalmen did not return. We did not learn of his whereabouts and of his physical condition until after the war.

After we had been confined in the Tornalya ghetto for several weeks, our Christian neighbors from Coltova paid us a visit. They inquired as to our needs and volunteered to bring us some essential items. By now, our food supplies had dwindled to a bare minimum. Bread was especially scarce, and we had no idea how long we would have to survive on the provisions we brought along. We were forced to ration bread. So we asked them to bring bread — plain, ordinary dry bread. They promised to do so, but we never heard from them again.

I have often contemplated the strange behavior of our former friends and neighbors. Perhaps the ruling regime had persuaded them by various means of propaganda and salesmanship to become passionate and zealous anti-Semites. Perhaps then, their visit was initiated to satiate their curiosity about life in the ghetto, rather than to assist us.

The possibility also exists that these people remained our staunch friends, but that they brought us no bread because they were prevented from doing so by the guards. Or perhaps they did not choose to display their friendship to Jews so openly for fear of reprisals by the regime. Thus, they might have been merely protecting themselves.

In the summer of 1996, while visiting Budapest, the capital of Hungary, my husband and I decided to take the 3 ½-hour trip to Coltova. When the Coltovians realized who I was, we were greeted with a rousing welcome. We hugged, we embraced, we kissed, we wept, and we laughed. They appeared so happy to see me again after a disappearance of 52 years.

My husband, who does not speak any Hungarian and based his judgment solely on the physical actions of these Coltovians, commented that he had never witnessed such a reception anywhere. These people certainly did not appear to be hostile to or discriminate against Jews, he added. Could they perhaps have been good actors and perpetrated a hoax on us? I really don't think so. This is especially true nowadays, when this territory has been returned to Slovakian sovereignty, and the population, mainly Hungarian, suffers undue discrimination at the hands of the Slovaks.

While in the ghetto, the mayor contacted me once again. He offered to take me out of the ghetto if I moved to his home and continue to spin the angora yarn. It was a most tempting offer, but considering the fact that I would have to leave my family if I accepted his offer, I had no choice but to turn it down. I could not leave my family in such troubled times, not knowing what the future had in store for us. At a time such as this, we would all stick together.

We had been confined to the Tornalya ghetto for approximately three weeks when it was suddenly announced that we were to pack our belongings and prepare for further travel. We were not informed of our ultimate destination. We boarded a train, which took us to the factory district of Dios Gyor, on the outskirts of Mishkolc, an important railroad junction in the northeastern section of Hungary, not too far from Tornalya. Many railroad lines converged at this station. We left the train and were ordered to sit on the ground. When night arrived, we were forced to sleep on a grassy area, without the comfort usually provided by mattresses, sheets, pillows, and blankets. All through the night we were guarded by rifle-carrying guards.

During the night, I overheard some soldiers discussing the fact that the Jews of Sanpeter would be shipped out that night. I quietly asked the soldiers about the whereabouts of these Sanpeter Jews. I followed their directions accurately and soon found my friend Marishka and her family members packing at a feverish pace. I helped them pack and they boarded the train. There, Marishka and I hugged, said our good-byes, and expressed the hope that we would meet again in better times. We never met again though, as Marishka perished in the concentration camps, one of the six million victims.

It was still dark when I returned to my family. My parents, who were already awake, appeared unusually frightened and extremely nervous. I was greeted with a feeling of relief and, at the same time, with extreme displeasure bordering on anger. Why had I caused such pain and agony by wandering away without consulting them? My attempted explanation that emotionally I felt it essential to bid good-bye to my Sanpeter friends, and that I was convinced that I would not be granted my parents' consent, proved to be of no avail. Although my father, as always, understood my feelings perfectly, he nevertheless posed a fair and legitimate question with a feeling of disappointment and frustration: "When did I ever forbid you to do anything you wanted and felt you had to do?" I further attempted to justify my behavior by telling my father that, unlike the past, we were now living in dangerous times. One could no longer rely on methods that had been effective in the past. Since I was well aware of my father's great love for me, I had assumed that he would have been too worried about my safety to have permitted me to go. The discussion ended when I fully agreed that my actions were wrong and that I sincerely regretted them.

In the morning, we were again ordered to board the trains for an, as yet, undeclared destination. Instead of regular trains constructed and equipped for the comfort and convenience of human beings, we were herded into cattle cars. The soldiers pushed so many people into these cars that conditions became extremely crowded, and there was hardly enough room even to sit on the floor. The doors were then bolted from the outside and our journey began.

At nightfall, we were all terribly exhausted, both physically and emotionally, yet we were unable to fall asleep. I asked my 5-year-old brother, Moshe Shmuel, to place his head on my lap, which he did, and finally he fell asleep.

An unusual case, which initiated strife and friction among the Jews in our car, occurred during the night. An elderly couple sat right next to us. The old man was very sick and since he knew that we had some water, he asked for it. My father reluctantly refused since it was incumbent upon him to save the water for his youngsters, my younger brothers and sister.

The Talmud discusses a situation in which two men are traveling on a journey far from civilization. One of them has a jug of water. If both drink, they will both die, since the jug does not contain a sufficient amount of water to sustain both. However, if only one drinks, he can reach civilization. *Halachically*, what should be done?

The son of Patura taught: It is better that both should drink and die, rather than one should behold his companion's death. However, Rabbi Akiva taught that since the Torah (in *Vayikra* 25:36) states, "That thy brother may live with thee," "וְחֵי אָחִיךָ עִמָּךְ," your own life takes precedence over his life.

The words "with thee" imply that your life takes priority, but that he too has a right to live after your own life is assured (*Bava Metzia* p. 62a).

In addition, Rabbi Yosef Karo, in his codes (*Yorah Deah* Ch. 251), explicitly teaches that one's own family's needs takes preference over the needs of all others (based on *Bava Metzia* p. 71a). Thus, my father's position could verily be substantiated from traditional *halachic* sources.

In spite of this, some voices in the cattle car were raised to challenge my father's position. Since my father wore the garb of an Orthodox Jew, everyone knew that he was a religious man. One individual in the car was so annoyed at my father's position that he severely castigated him. He told him, "You are a religious man, and yet you refuse to give a little water to a sick man? Has the Torah taught you nothing?" My father chose not to respond. He was certainly not in the mood to quarrel with a suffering, well-meaning Jew, who was experiencing the same misery and agony that had become our own lot in life.

All the commotion in the car woke my brother Moshe, who then graciously offered me his lap. "I was able to sleep awhile on your lap," he said, "so now you place your head on my lap, so that you too can get some sleep." He was such a loving and affectionate young boy.

It was an appalling and horrifying night. The heat and humidity were unbearable. Because of the lack of any toilet facilities, the resulting stench created a most nauseating and highly polluted atmosphere in the car. The death of a man during the night increased the already significant stench and further contaminated and defiled our cramped quarters. The seemingly long and arduous night eventually came to an end. Finally, the train stopped and the doors were unbolted. Hardly anyone in the car attempted to leave. My sister Fayge and I slowly made our way to the door for a gasp of fresh air. Reading some of the many posted signs and placards at the station, I realized that we were still in Hungarian territory. Everything appeared to be in the Hungarian language. However, I was unable to identify our exact geographic location. I did not recognize the name of the town and somehow it really didn't interest me at the time.

I then noticed several water pumps not too far away. I begged the patrolling soldiers to permit Fayge and me to leave the train to fetch some drinking water. They initially turned down my request. I felt that their negative response was due to their concern that I would take advantage of the opportunity to escape. I assured them that the idea of escaping never entered my mind. Where would I go in my exhausted and fatigued physical condition? I then invited them to escort me to the pumps. They then granted permission to us both to go to the pumps. They emphasized, however, that we must return immediately.

We then asked our fellow passengers to give us their empty jugs and containers, offering to bring them as much water as we could possibly carry. I do not remember how many round trips we made to the pumps, but I can vividly recall that our fellow travelers greatly appreciated our aid, for it enabled them to quench their thirst.

Suddenly, my father's popularity began to rise dramatically. Some reasoned that if my father had been able to raise such good-hearted daughters, he himself must be a virtuous and highly ethical individual. Some even offered their most sincere apologies for having reproached him. My father's response reflected his typical modesty and deep humility. He certainly bore no malice nor malevolence toward any individual on the train. They were all concerned, well-intentioned Jews. In fact, he told them, he himself was burdened with a sense of guilt, because he had been unable to help a sick man.

Our troubles were just beginning. For several more days (I no longer recall the exact number), we continued to survive

Area near Auschwitz

in our cramped quarters on the train, which appeared to be traveling at a most leisurely pace.

The food supplies we brought from the ghetto were dwindling rapidly. Since we had no idea how long these supplies would have to last, we consumed them sparingly. However, nobody appeared to be hungry and certainly nobody had any particular cravings for food. Amidst the heat and foul air, our appetites had disappeared completely. However, our captors brought no food or water onto the train. As far as they were concerned, we could all perish. They couldn't care less. In fact, an additional number of people died during the long and arduous journey, but the train did not stop.

THE TRAIN FINALLY CAME TO A HALT. THE DOORS opened, and we heard German soldiers shouting frantically,

Arrival at Auschwitz

"Raus schnell! — Get out of the train quickly!" We stumbled out of the train and were suddenly dazed by the powerful rays of the June sunshine. Having been confined for several days in the dark-

The selection area near the entrance to Auschwitz

ness of the cattle cars, it took us some time to become adjusted to the bright sunlight again.

One by one, we were pushed along until we reached a man dressed in military garb, wearing white gloves. He appeared to be in complete charge. He waved some people to the right and others to the left. My father, my brother, and my older sister were waved to the right whereas my mother, I, and the rest of the family were waved to the left.

My mother suddenly began to scream hysterically. "We're all going to be killed! Oh my God, they are going to kill us all!" I was overcome emotionally. I could not bear hearing so much talk of death when I so much wanted to live. So I covered my ears, ever so tightly.

"How old are you?" I was asked by an approaching soldier, who spoke in Hungarian. When I informed him of my age, he immediately yelled at me. "You are supposed to go to the right! Turn around and go back!" He then proceeded to push me toward the right with his rifle. My younger sister was treated in a similar manner. We both ran back and caught up with our older sister. There was no hope of catching up with my father

Hungarian women arriving in Auschwitz in the summer of 1944

and brother as, by now, the sexes had already been separated. We were now officially inmates of Auschwitz.

We later discovered that a wave to the left indicated that the individual was considered unfit for work and was thus destined for immediate death in the gas chambers. All children, old people, sick, crippled, and weak Jews, and all pregnant women were included in that group.

Who was this man who, with the flick of his finger, decreed life or death? It was, in all probability, the infamous Joseph Mengele (or one of his appointed henchmen), who has become one of the symbols of the Holocaust and has been referred to by the camp inmates as the "Auschwitz monster" or the "Angel of Death." He is specifically known for his nefarious, degenerate medical experiments on living Jews, whom he took from the barracks and brought to his hospital block. In many instances, he used the pretext of medical treatment to kill prisoners personally, injecting them with chloroform or petrol, or ordering SS medical orderlies to do so.

> *One of the few people to speak to Mengele in Auschwitz about his attitude to the Jews was a Christian woman, Dr. Ella Lingens. She had been deported to Auschwitz from Vienna three months before Mengele's own arrival in the camp, having been denounced for sheltering Jews and for helping them escape across the Austrian border into Switzerland. She later recalled how, in Auschwitz, she was in a triply privileged position, as a German, as a non-Jew, and as a doctor. During one of his conversations with her, Mengele said that there were only two gifted nations in the world — the Germans and the Jews. The question is, which one will dominate?*
>
> *Ella Lingens later recalled an example of Mengele's ruthlessness. After all efforts to contain an outbreak of spotted fever had failed, he ordered the entire block cleared by sending all of its 600 or 700 inmates to the gas chambers. Then he had the barracks disinfected and populated by the thoroughly deloused prisoners of another block. The process, delousing and gassing, was repeated many times until the spotted fever was brought under control.*

Having been selected to join the group to the right, we were all taken to a large room with a cement floor. We were then ordered to remove all of our clothing. Pitchers of water were brought in and a pushing scene ensued as everyone was most anxious to get to the water. I never even made the effort to reach the water. Being smaller than most girls, I surmised that such an effort would be fruitless.

Over the next few hours my appearance changed dramatically. We were ordered to stand in line to have our hair cut. Seven Jewish girls, themselves prisoners at the concentration camp, stood with hair clippers in their hands and proceeded to cut our hair. Everyone's hair was completely shaved off. My pleas to one of these girls to leave just a little were completely ignored. In fact, she advised me not to worry about my hair. I should be more concerned about my life, she pointed out.

A dreadful, frightful thought now entered my mind. Was the girl's remark a statement of reality? Was this the future we could all anticipate? Were we to experience a daily struggle for our very existence? Or was the young lady was merely exaggerating? Little did I know at the time.

With these thoughts haunting my mind, we were sent to the showers. After the many ordeals we were subjected to ever since we entered the ghetto on approximately May 20, we surely welcomed the showers on June 15. Although we were now the prisoners of a barbaric and savage Nazi regime, the showers did succeed in refreshing us, at least physically.

One-piece gray dresses of sackcloth were now distributed to us. There were no undergarments included in this "gift." The dress I received did not fit, as it was probably many sizes too large. At this stage, we were returned to the large room with the concrete floor, and were ordered to sit, pull up our knees, fold our arms around our knees, and immediately go to sleep. Exhausted from a long and arduous day, it was no wonder that I fell asleep immediately.

The hysterical scream of *"Raus — appell!"* woke us at 4:30 a.m. We were ordered to go outside. We were lined up in rows of five and the roll call of camp inmates began. The counting lasted for several long hours and it was quite a rigorous stint. The hot June sun shone brightly in the morning and created havoc with our skin. It severely burned our shaved heads and bare legs. Our captors, well aware of our painful encounter with the sun, showed little concern about our plight and predicament. Why should they? Weren't they completely covered and protected from the sun's rays? Who cared about the Jews?

Again, we stood in line, this time for breakfast. We received black coffee, a thick and heavy hunk of black bread, and a bit of margarine. The bread not only resembled mud due to its slimy and heavy texture, but it also tasted like mud. Our initial reaction was to cast the bread away. However, some girls, who had arrived at the camp before our own arrival, asked us to give them our share and, of course, we did. They assured us that the next day, we too would consume the bread despite its taste. They were right. The next day, our hunger was so severe that we ate the bread. Taste no longer seemed to matter. Hunger became our prime concern.

We were then assigned to our living quarters in the barracks. Each barrack, which housed more than 150 inmates, was furnished with bunk beds containing several tiers of berths one above another. The beds were supplied with mattresses and blankets. There were several toilet facilities available, though certainly not an adequate number for such a huge throng of humans, and running water was plentiful. This was to be the first time that we would be able to sleep in beds since we left Coltova.

In the afternoon, we were again lined up for a several-hour *appell* stint, which was followed by supper. The meal contained a thick mixture of unknown ingredients resembling a cereal. Its flavor was disgusting, totally repugnant and obnoxious to our taste. Many nearly choked as they consumed this dish. But what could we do? We had no alternatives but to partake of this food. Nobody wanted to face the consequences of malnutrition. My sister Golde can distinctly recall that several young girls actually fainted due to lack of sufficient food.

Ever since we had entered the Auschwitz grounds, I was under the strong impression that we had been brought here for the purpose of labor. With so many Germans actively involved in the military aspects of the war, being forced to fight the Allies on several fronts, there was a severe shortage of manpower on the domestic front. I strongly believed that we were selected to fill this vacuum. Any day now, I thought, we would be joining working units in the vicinity of Auschwitz.

A huge sign at Auschwitz's front gate clearly states in large letters, *"Arbeit Macht Frei"* — work makes one free. I always imagined that the purpose of the sign was to motivate us, to offer us incentives to pursue our working responsibilities rigorously.

However, much to my astonishment, our working orders in Auschwitz never came. Was there perhaps another yet more sinister reason for our presence in Auschwitz? I wondered. They certainly did not send us here as their honored guests just to participate in a twice-daily *appell* and to consume two daily luscious meals at the luxurious Hotel Auschwitz.

Another Move

AFTER WE SPENT NINE DAYS IN AUSCHWITZ, WE WERE ordered to march to the railroad station to board another cattle train. This time, our destination was Plasov, Poland, on the outskirts of Crakow. Each one of us was immediately given an injection, for a reason unknown to any of us at the time. I can now reasonably assume that the injections were given to prevent normal bodily functions.

In Plasov, we were assigned to a work unit near a huge garbage dump. It became our task to rake the scattered garbage into large piles. Wheelbarrows then brought it to waiting trucks. It was drizzling slightly at the time. A bridge had been constructed over the dump and I noticed several women, wearing plastic raincoats in various colors, crossing it. From my vantage point, these raincoats appeared to be extremely beautiful. Engrossed and absorbed in my thoughts, I began to daydream. Why am I here? Why am I not in Coltova with my family? Why are those women there?

A sharp slap on my face by a male *Kapo* shocked me back to reality. The blow was so powerful that it threw me onto the ground. "Here we don't dream, here we work!" the *Kapo* screamed. I will always remember that day, as it marked the first time I was struck in a concentration camp. More physical violence, of course, was yet to come.

The administration of the concentration camp consisted of prisoners who were chosen to act as an elder, a camp clerk, and a "Chief of Labor Statistics." They, in turn, divided each camp into blocks, assigned to block elders, block clerks, and a group of *Kapos*. The *Kapo*-in-chief was generally a German prisoner serving a sentence for a nonpolitical crime.

With the growth of the camp population after the outbreak of the war, there were also some Jews among the *Kapos* assigned to the block. Since the major qualifications for a leading position in the camp was one's ability to be brutal, it is evident that many of the Jewish *Kapos* were individuals who could boast of some crimes committed before detention in the camps or who had become known for terrorizing fellow prisoners.

The fate of all *Kapos* was certain death. They functioned for three to four months and then were sent to the crematorium, while others took their place. The inmates of the camps, with some rare exceptions, generally despised the Jewish *Kapos*. How could Jews turn against their own suffering brethren and often treat them in an even more brutal fashion than some Nazis themselves? How could Jews have sunk to such a low level? In my own eyes, many of the *Kapos* were beneath contempt.

It should be noted at this point that during the entire 10-month period that we were imprisoned in the concentration camps (from June 15, 1944 to April 15, 1945), we were never offered the convenience of eating at a table while seated on a chair. "Standard operating procedure" required us to pick up a metal dish and join an ever growing line. When our turn finally came, kitchen attendants would fill the dish, which we would bring into the barracks, to be consumed on our beds.

Although the meager amount of food we received in Plasov was of inferior quality and certainly far from adequate to supply the nutritional requirements of the camp inmates, it was, however, a slight improvement over the Auschwitz standards. Here, a supper included a tiny piece of meat and some potatoes. Not being familiar with the *halachic* requirements pertaining to kosher food in our present circumstances, while so many of us were sick and feeble, bordering on starvation, we nevertheless abstained from the meat.

One particular day, when we were suffering from severe hunger pangs, I began to wonder whether perhaps there was a way to surreptitiously enter the kitchen facilities to obtain some vitally needed food. We should certainly make the effort, I felt. When I mentioned this possibility to my younger sister, she was quite apprehensive about this project. "The Nazis have posted guards at the kitchen doors and we will most certainly be caught," she reasoned. However, due to the ever increasing hunger pangs we were enduring at the time, she consented to join me in the venture.

When we arrived in the kitchen area, we noticed immediately that an armed soldier stood right in front of the door. We decided to hide in the bushes to see what he would do. After a short while, when the soldier walked into the kitchen, I decided to follow him. There was a distance of no more than two or three feet separating us. I noticed some food on the table, grabbed it quickly, and left the kitchen area.

I returned to the bushes and found my sister trembling with fear. She was seized with trepidation and could hardly talk. Finally, she cried hysterically, "If that Nazi soldier had turned around and noticed you following him at such close range, he surely would have shot you on the spot! If he had apprehended you with the food, he undoubtedly would have ended your life right then and there. Do you think he was carrying his gun merely as a toy?"

Never again would she participate in such a risky project, she assured me. She would rather die of malnutrition than join in any such covert adventure. With my sister still trembling, we returned to our barracks. My older sister then suggested that perhaps I should now recite *"birchas hagomel,"* thanking Hashem for having saved me from a dangerous situation.

Electrified fence separating men from women at Auschwitz

Existing under the horrendous conditions of the camps made the process of degradation of the "inner person" inevitable. Many inmates could not resist the temptation to employ any opportunistic device to gain the necessities to make survival possible. On the other hand, many prisoners found the courage to tolerate the horrors of camp life and even to render some aid to their friends. Such small, self-sacrificing acts helped the prisoners to remain human.

AFTER SPENDING SIX WEEKS LABORING IN PLASOV, we were marched back to the station, where cattle trains were

Return to Auschwitz waiting to return us to Auschwitz. This time, we remained in Auschwitz for a period of 10 days. As in our prior stay, we were not assigned to any work units and we had no specific task to perform. Mainly, we stood in line twice daily for roll calls and we partook of our regular meals, such as they were.

A most unexpected occurrence transpired on our second day back in Auschwitz. As my sisters and I were sitting near a high-voltage barbed wire fence, which separated the women's area from the men's area, we heard several men communicating in Hungarian. It suddenly occurred to me that perhaps our father was part of this group. Excitedly, we walked to the fence, where we observed several men sitting on the ground working rigorously to chop huge boulders into smaller stones.

I called out to the men, "Hello! Does anyone here know somebody named Yaakov Herskovits from Tornalya?"

We were flabbergasted when one man responded affirmatively. "Yaakov Herskovits is the one who usually arranges a *minyan* for us whenever possible," he told us. How typical of my father to do this, I thought, even under such conditions!

"Please," I begged, "bring him over here, as we are his three daughters and we are most anxious to see him."

"That's impossible," the man responded, "Yaakov Herskovits is too young to have three grown-up daughters."

Upon our insistence that he might indeed be our father, the man volunteered to change places with him. "I shall work at his station, and he can come to the fence to work at my station. As long as the work continues at its normal pace, no supervising officer will ever discover the change."

The man left. I felt so tense and high strung that every minute seemed like hours. Would we see our father soon? What was his physical and mental condition? Would he bring us news of our brother, Chaim Leib?

As my eyes inadvertently turned in the direction of the kitchen, I noticed a crate of cabbages standing right next to its entrance. In my hungry state, I eagerly began walking toward the kitchen with the resolved intention of taking just one cabbage. How good that would taste! Yet before I had the opportunity to place my hand upon a cabbage, I noticed my younger sister running toward me, excitedly shouting, "*Tatty* is here! *Tatty* is here!" Without the slightest hesitation, I ran back to the fence.

There was my father sitting on the ground, chopping boulders into stones. He looked so thin and weak that he appeared much younger than his 47 years. There was a smile on his lips, yet tears were rolling from his eyes. He told me that his heart had skipped a beat when he didn't see me at first.

We then began to talk in earnest. Sometimes he was able to obtain a newspaper, he told us, and he recently read that the Russian army's rapid advance had brought it extremely close to Auschwitz. He felt that the war would be over soon, and that the day of our liberation was near. He had also heard that mothers and their young children were being held in a more civilized camp, where the food was better in quality and in quantity, he told us encouragingly.

When we informed him that we were refraining from eating the *treife* meat, he responded, "My dear children, you are permitted to eat everything. Otherwise, you may not survive. Did the Torah itself not teach us (*Vayikra* 18:5), 'And thou shalt live by them' — 'וָחַי בָּהֶם'?" Except for three cardinal sins (idolatry, adultery, and murder), the law of saving one's life supersedes all laws of the Torah. One may certainly eat *treife* meat in order to save one's life (*Yoma* 85a and b)."

My father then informed us that he believed that there would be a selection for transportation to other places. There would be many groups. Rumors were spreading that some groups would be sent to better places than others. He advised us to make no attempt to change to any other group, but to always remain where they placed us. However, he warned us, if we were ever separated, we should expend every effort to get together again. "United, your chances for survival will vastly improve because you will assist each other and encourage each other." In this section of Auschwitz, he told us, only people eventually sent to other places were confined. As a matter of fact, my father said, he expected to be leaving Auschwitz the next day.

Above all, my father insisted that we must never lose hope. "With hope you will survive," he assured us. "Even if a sharp sword rests upon a man's neck, he should not desist from prayer [אֲפִילוּ חֶרֶב חַדָּה מוּנַחַת עַל צַוָּארוֹ שֶׁל אָדָם אַל יִמְנַע עַצְמוֹ מִן הָרַחֲמִים (*Berachos* 10a)]. The help of Hashem can be immediate. It can arrive as quickly as the wink of an eye, even amidst the raging inferno of Nazism. So you must continue to hope and pray," he concluded.

A screaming female *Kapo* suddenly interrupted our conversation. "Get away from the fence!" she yelled. "If that man's *Kapo* will see him talking to you, he will be severely beaten!"

Our father asked us to return to the fence area later that afternoon, when he would be lined up for the *appell* and we would be able to see each other again.

The female *Kapo* turned out to be a rarity among Jewish *Kapos*. Despite her gruff exterior, she was a good-natured woman with a pleasant and kind disposition. She possessed a warm heart and a genuine *yiddishe neshamah*. When we explained to her that the man we were talking to was none other than our own father, she became extremely excited and was most anxious to hear additional details. How had we managed to find our father?

She, of course, was fully aware of the fact that we had missed the lunch meal and she reassured us that together we would go into the kitchen to obtain some food. Virtually all of the girls working in the kitchen were overwhelmed when the *Kapo* related our experience to them. They were all extremely interested to learn more of the details while they were serving us more food than we had ever received before at a concentration camp.

Late in the afternoon, we returned to the fence area and witnessed our father standing in line for the roll call. When he saw us and began to walk to our direction, the *Kapo* who had followed him punched him with such force that he fell to the ground. We screamed along with him in agony and pain. It is unbearable to see your own father being physically abused with such brute force and have to stand by helplessly. My father immediately jumped back to his feet and while hastening back to his row in the *appell*, he turned slightly and waved to us as if to say, "It's all right. I'm fine."

Meanwhile, our kind *Kapo* ran to us screaming, "Didn't I warn you not to talk to the men? This poor man was beaten because of you!" We felt horrible and we cried bitterly. Then we left the area. When we returned some time later in the day, our father was no longer there. We never saw him again.

On the following day, we were sitting on the ground between the *appells* and between meals, seriously discussing our plight. What was happening to us? If anyone would ever describe inhumane treatment of people similar to the treatment we were being subjected to, who would believe him? If we ever got out alive from this hellhole of torment and wickedness and then related our experiences to others, we would most certainly be branded insane lunatics, suffering from severe hallucinations. Of course, we would be told that no matter how ferocious and how barbaric one individual might have been, no human could be capable of committing such horrendous crimes as we were ascribing to the Nazis.

A Polish girl, sitting nearby, overheard our conversation. "You have just arrived in Auschwitz," she said, "so you don't know anything yet. I have been here for years." She then pointed to a huge smoking chimney in the distance. "Just look at the chimney," she told us. "What do you think they are burning in the furnace below?" She then answered her own question by informing us that they probably had already burned the rest of our family by then. "They burn all those who have been declared unfit for work," she informed us. She concluded by expressing her most fervent hope and prayer that we all would not end up there.

This was the first time we had ever heard that in Auschwitz, human beings were being torched by flames. The

Crematorium furnaces

girl's talk made me extremely nervous, although my sisters and I had difficulty believing a word she said. We felt that this was an embittered young girl who had suffered so much during the past several years that she had lost all hope and had absolutely nothing to look forward to. Naturally, we sympathized with her and made efforts to allay her many fears.

Of course, the girl's account of the transpiring events proved to be indubitably accurate. After January 20, 1942, when the means for the "final solution" were decided upon, the major concentration camps became "*Vernichtungslagern*" — annihilation camps. Chief among them was Auschwitz, which was distinguished for achieving the greatest efficiency in the process of exterminating men, women, and children. It eventually boasted a record of 6,000 people put to death per day.

It was in these camps that medical experiments were conducted: research into the origin and causes of dual births, the causes of birth of dwarfs and giants, and the treatment of uncommon diseases. Inmates were used as human guinea pigs. Much of the research was done through dissection of corpses. There was no dearth of them in Auschwitz.

At the Nuremberg trials of the war criminals after the German surrender, it was reported that the greatest and most notorious of the death camps was Auschwitz, whose four huge gas chambers and adjoining crematoria gave it a capacity for death and burial far beyond all others. One of the camp's commanders for a period was Rudolf Hoess, an ex-convict once found guilty of murder, who deposed at Nuremberg about the superiority of the gas he employed.

He testified that he had visited the Treblinka death camp to find out how they carried out their extermination of the Jews of Europe. The camp commandant told him that he had liquidated 80,000 in the course of half a year. He was principally concerned with liquidating all the Jews from the Warsaw Ghetto. In Treblinka, however, carbon monoxide gas was used, and Hoess did not think that this method was very efficient. So when he set up the extermination building in Auschwitz, he used Zyklon B, a crystallized prussic acid which was dropped into the death chamber from a small opening. It took from three to fifteen minutes to kill all the people in the death chamber, depending upon climatic conditions.

Hoess also boasted that in Auschwitz, the gas chambers were constructed to accommodate 2,000 people at one time, whereas the 10 gas chambers in Treblinka accommodated only 200 people each.

Although at the time of selection at the Auschwitz railroad station, heartrending scenes occurred as wives were torn away from husbands and children from parents, none of the captives, Hoess testified, realized just what was in store for them. In fact, some of them were given pretty picture postcards marked "Waldsee" to be signed and sent back home to their relatives with a printed inscription, saying: "We are doing very well here. We have work and we are well treated. We await your arrival."

I can definitely attest to the accuracy of Hoess' statement. At the time, however, none of us took the Polish girl's account seriously. It was simply too incomprehensible.

It was during the early days of the month of August that we were confined in Auschwitz. We hadn't enjoyed a decent meal since we departed from Coltova 2½ months earlier. Hunger was becoming a real problem. Regular rumblings in my stomach clearly indicated that more food was an urgent need. My cravings for any type of food continued uninterruptedly as my physical condition weakened considerably.

I decided to make another attempt to go to the kitchen. Near the outside wall of the kitchen, the Nazis had stored many types of fresh vegetables, and I planned to help myself to some of those delicacies. How good that would make me feel!

When I attempted to snatch a cabbage from a crate, a Nazi suddenly appeared upon the scene and slapped my face so hard that I was thrown to the ground. The blow was so powerful that it injured my ear and for days, my hearing was impaired.

I then told my sisters that the Nazi who so violently slapped me reminded me of a mad dog. Though I was hurt physically, my feelings were not hurt. Like a heroine, I then most emphatically declared that I would not weep over the incident. However, shortly thereafter, I found myself sobbing uncontrollably. This incident also caused me, at least for a while, to lose some of my tenacity in my effort to obtain food for my sisters and for myself.

One day, the inmates of several barracks were marched to the bathhouses for much needed showers. We were told to remove all of our clothes and stand in the hot, burning sun while a hundred girls at a time used the showers. Finally, it was our turn to shower. We were able to shower, get dressed, and return to the barracks in lines of five. We were now lined up for supper. After receiving a meager soup of unknown ingredients, a group of girls arrived from the showers. They were extremely thirsty and begged us for some water to quench their thirst. I immediately took my water-filled dish and brought it to them. Unfortunately, when the *Kapo* noticed me standing near the newly arrived girls, she accused me of attempting to stand in line again for an extra portion of food. My unequivocal denial of the charges, corroborated by the girls who received the water, was of no avail. The *Kapo* slapped me in the face and when I fell to the ground, she continued my punishment by kicking me mercilessly.

Near the end of our Auschwitz confinement, my sister Golde was assigned to a different group. Fortunately, she was able to avoid the ever watchful eye of the Gestapo and speedily returned to us. This happened on three different occasions — we were separated at first, but following our father's final directive to us, eventually we were able to come together again. We made every effort to remain united throughout our entire ordeal. In this area, at least, our efforts were crowned with success.

One more chore had to be performed before we left Auschwitz. Each one of us was assigned a specific number, which was tattooed onto our left arm. My number was A-19470. It remains affixed on my arm to this day.

Many Auschwitz survivors have seen fit to remove the number by surgery upon the conclusion of the war. However, my husband's rebbe, the renowned Gaon Harav Eliezer Silver zt"l of Cincinnati, had strongly urged that these numbers remain on our arms forever to serve as a constant reminder of the unprovoked persecutions and atrocities committed against the Jews by the Nazi regime. This would also be in compliance with the Biblical command, "Remember what Amalek did unto you on the way, as you came out of Egypt…you shall not forget!" (Devarim 25:17,19). "זָכוֹר אֵת אֲשֶׁר עָשָׂה לְךָ עֲמָלֵק בַּדֶּרֶךְ בְּצֵאתְכֶם מִמִּצְרָיִם ... לֹא תִּשְׁכָּח" *Rav Silver quoted the opinion of the Vilna Gaon, that Germany has the possible status of Amalek.*

When Kaiser Wilhelm of Germany visited Eretz Yisrael in the year 1899, many of Jerusalem's residents went out to greet him. They were most anxious to recite the blessing which is recited upon seeing a king (Berachos 58a). "בָּרוּךְ שֶׁנָּתַן מִכְּבוֹדוֹ לִבְרִיּוֹתָיו" *However, the eminent Gaon Harav Yosef Chaim Sonnenfeld*

R' Yosef Chaim Sonnenfeld

remained at home and did not participate in the official reception for the Kaiser, stating that no blessing is recited when seeing a king descended from Amalek, and that according to the Vilna Gaon, Germany has the possible status of Amalek.

The sefer Yalkut Me'am Loez states that when we read in the Passover Haggadah, "In every generation they rise up against us to destroy us," "שֶׁבְּכָל דּוֹר וָדוֹר עוֹמְדִים עָלֵינוּ לְכַלּוֹתֵנוּ", we are referring to Amalek, who in every generation is embodied in a different nation. Thus, all enemies of the Jews are included in the mitzvah of remembering Amalek.

"Grant not, Hashem, the desires of the wicked one: do not grant his conspiracy fruition" — "אַל תִּתֵּן ה' מַאֲוַיֵּי רָשָׁע זְמָמוֹ אַל תָּפֵק..." (Tehillim 140:9). The Talmud states (in Megillah 6b) that this is a reference to Germamya of Edom: "If they were permitted to roam freely, they would destroy the entire world." Amalek was a descendant of Edom (Bereishis 36:12). More than two centuries ago, the renowned sage, Harav Yaakov Emden, stated, in his commentary on the Talmud, that this Talmudic text is a reference to Germany. One can easily note the striking resemblance between the name Germany and "Germamya" mentioned in the Talmud. Thus, the commandment "to remember Amalek" applies to Germany today.

CHAPTER 5
GUBEN AND BERGEN-BELSEN

GAIN WE MARCHED TO THE RAILROAD station to be herded into cattle trains. We had no inkling as to our destination. After a long and arduous journey, we arrived in a factory district, where we could see some army barracks in the distance. There was the usual roll call. Upon its completion, we were taken to the barracks, where each one of us was assigned to a bunk bed, which was to become our sleeping and living space for the duration of our stay. The barracks were unusually clean. They were even equipped with lavatories and showers. There were as many as five lavatories in our barracks.

The gray sackcloth dresses we received in Auschwitz were now exchanged for civilian clothing. Each one of us received a dress, a coat, and a pair of wooden shoes. Each one also received a numbered tag, which we were to wear around our necks all day. (Since the numbers on the tag and the numbers on my arm did not match, and the tag numbers were never used, I have often wondered about the purpose of issuing these tag numbers in the first place.)

We had now reached a point in our lives when our names had become totally irrelevant. Just like convicts in a penitentiary or animals grazing in the meadows, we had no names. Only numbers identified us. When the Gestapo guards summoned us for any specific purpose, they always addressed us by a number, rather than a name. We had lost our special identity as human beings. We were nothing more than numbers.

According to Jewish law, it is forbidden to count the Jews by assigning a specific number to each one (*Yoma* 22b). In order to ascertain whether 10 people are present for the purpose of establishing a *minyan*, we recite a Biblical verse containing 10 words and each individual is then assigned a specific word. When a census of the Israelites was taken in the Sinai desert, each Jew contributed a coin, one half of a *shekel*, and the coins were then counted. Perhaps such a system was used to impress us with the vital fact that a person is not to be treated merely as a number. Every person is a human being possessing his or her own name and special identity.

We arrived at Guben in the latter half of August 1944, and we were to remain there until early March 1945, when we began our long march to the Bergen-Belsen death camp. It is difficult to cite exact dates, since during our entire confinement period we had no access to any calendars. In Bergen-Belsen, though, we will always remember the date of April 15, when we were liberated by the British army.

In Guben we worked the night shift. We worked with fine wires and with metal spools. We were never informed, however, of the purpose of our labors. Working conditions in Guben were far from adequate. Food supplies were so limited and of such inferior quality that some of the girls often lost consciousness from malnutrition. They were much too frail and infirm to perform the rigorous physical labors required at the wire factory. During the daytime hours we all should have been sleeping to rest our tired bodies and to regain our physical strength for another working night. However, sleeping was easier said than done. The wooden barracks were never heated. As a matter of fact, heating facilities in the barracks did not even exist. The temperature in the cold German winter was usually below freezing. So who could really spend a restful and tranquil day under such conditions?

Since each of us had only one light blanket, my sisters and I decided to amalgamate and merge our worldly assets. We resolved that all three of us should sleep in the same bunk bed, using all three blankets, and gaining additional warmth from each other's body heat. Our sleeping quarters were quite cramped but the heat crisis was, at least, partially alleviated.

How I had always loathed working for the Nazis! Why should I labor for a nation of anti-Semites, whose members boasted of being part of the so-called master race, while they considered us such lowly creatures? It vexed me terribly that they were able to wield so much power over us. We labored in their factories while they paid for our services by humiliating and persecuting us. They did not even provide us with our basic living requirements. Our stomachs were never satisfied, as we always felt severe hunger pangs. I abhorred those Nazis.

I thought that perhaps I could create something with the wires with which we worked, and then barter the product of my creation for some additional food for my sisters and myself. There were some heavier, stiff wires on the working tables. I began experimenting with those wires. The fine wires on the table came in three colors: green, bronze, and silver. I first wrapped the fine bronze wire around the heavier wire and noticed that it became curly. I then wrapped the green wire around the heavier wire and was able to create something resembling the stem of a flower. I then shaped the curly wire into a flower, and attached it to the stem. The fine green wires were then shaped into leaves and I attached these to the stem as well. I completed my work by creating a pin with the heavier wire. The end result was a flower pin.

I discovered that with these wires, other items could be created. I began shaping the wires into a French poodle, a rabbit, and a reindeer with horns.

The camp's cook was delighted to see the items I had created, and was more than happy to give me some food for them. It was with a great feeling of satisfaction and with a prayer of thanks to Hashem that I brought the food into the barracks to share with my sisters. My older sister, Fayge, was selected to divide it among the three of us, and she made sure that each one received an equal share. Despite the additional food, we were still extremely hungry, but at least we had achieved progress in our ongoing battle against starvation.

The barracks were divided into several rooms. Each room housed 30 girls on bunk beds. Since the lavatories were at the far side of the barracks, it was quite difficult to reach it on a winter night, when the temperature dropped below the freezing level. The barracks, which resembled sheds or barns, were certainly not insulated to protect us from the outside elements, and icy cold winds were free to blow in at random. In addition, we had only scanty clothing at our disposal, nothing more than a thin dress, a light spring coat, and a pair of wooden shoes. To alleviate the problem, one girl was able to obtain a pail, which we placed near our sleeping quarters. This pail could be used by each of us during the night, and we would no longer have to take the long and dreadful trip to the lavatories. We agreed that each morning another girl would empty the pail. All agreed to participate in this distasteful, yet useful procedure, except my sister Golde. She considered this chore to be utterly repugnant to her. She simply felt that she could not handle such an obnoxious task. She preferred to brave the cold weather and trek to the lavatories at the far side of the barracks.

One particular morning, my sister hurried to the lavatory, carrying her dish, which was ordinarily used for the purpose of obtaining food. She carefully placed the dish on a ledge outside, clearly intending to use it upon leaving for the ritual washing of her hands, as required by Jewish law. When the ever vigilant eye of a *Kapo* observed her haste in returning to her sleeping quarters, she immediately accused her of transporting waste products in her food dish. This is highly unsanitary, my sister was apprised. It could create a health epidemic of major proportions in the Guben camp.

My sister's attempts at denial proved to be useless, as the *Kapo* insisted that she witnessed the entire act. "I never make mistakes," she proudly declared. "I caught you red-handed!" She proceeded to jot down my sister's number and promised to lodge a complaint against her with the Gestapo.

The customary punishment meted out for any violations of the Gestapo camp code was severe and rigorous, indeed. The accused individual was forced to stand barefoot in the snow, without even the partial warmth provided by a coat. When the individual eventually collapsed and became unconscious, it marked the termination of his or her punishment, and he or she was considered to have paid the required debt to the Gestapo society. It should be pointed out that in our weakened physical condition at the time, we could not possible survive such a cruel punishment. Therefore, the punishment awaiting my sister was, in reality, nothing less than a death sentence.

Obviously, this certainly was not a pleasant way to begin another day of torture and agony at the "Guben Health Center." We were greatly distressed as we slowly made our way to another *appell*.

In the presence of Gestapo officers, the *Kapo* stood arrogantly in front of the entire group, ready to discipline my sister. She was prepared to teach her the lesson of her life — literally. We were all overcome with panic and our bodies trembled as she haughtily began announcing my sister's number. Suddenly we realized that she had failed to copy the number correctly. The last numeral did not match. We immediately advised my sister not to respond. After all, her number had not been announced. Several additional announcements of the erroneous number bore no results for the *Kapo*.

The frustrated *Kapo* then personally began to check out the entire group where inmates were lined up in rows of five. She hysterically walked up and down the aisles to apprehend the vicious criminal. Since my sister was shorter than the other four girls in our row, we were able to hide her from the *Kapo*'s view. Her intentions to punish and chastise an innocent victim having failed, the defeated *Kapo* departed from the *appell*, her face contorted with rage and fury. Certainly she felt that this was not over, that it was not the end. She would catch her yet.

When we returned to the barracks, the entire incident was fully related and explained to the 30 girls in the room. No one actually believed the veracity of the charges. All were firmly convinced that my sister never transported waste products in a food dish, thereby endangering everyone's health and well-being. Everyone then unanimously agreed that should the *Kapo* insist on filing a false report with the Gestapo, all would readily testify on behalf of my sister.

When we later arrived for work at the factory, the *Kapo* immediately recognized my sister. "Here you are! This time I got you!" she triumphantly exclaimed. "Why did you not step forward when I called your number at the *appell*?"

When my sister vacillated, I decided to answer for her. "You never announced her number," I confidently replied. "Just look at the number you jotted down and compare it with the number on my sister's arm. They do not match. You did not see the number correctly and you also never saw my sister transporting waste products. It never happened."

When she insisted that she knew what she saw, I informed her that I had 30 witnesses prepared to testify that she was mistaken. These witnesses knew that my sister always carried the empty food dish to the lavatories solely for the purpose of washing her hands, in compliance with *halachah*.

I then began to speak in German, which I had learned back in my hometown of Coltova. "As you see," I told the *Kapo*, "I, too, can converse in German. If I tell the Nazis, with 30 witnesses supporting me, that you are mistaken, who do you think they will believe? Remember, despite the fact that you are actually assisting them in the torture and persecution of your own fellow Jews, in the eyes of the Nazis you are nothing more than a lowly, bedraggled, and ordinary Jew. You are but a dilapidated creature, who, up to now, has been tolerated in the land of the so-called Master Race." The *Kapo* listened intently to my words of caution and desisted from any further moves against my sister.

Although living conditions in Guben were vastly superior to the living conditions in other places to which we had been confined in the past, we still suffered from hunger and from the cold arctic weather. Though showers were available, the cement floor under the showers was always covered with a thick layer of ice. So we stood on the ice, barefoot and naked, to shower daily in the morning. There were no towels available for us. It was no wonder, therefore, that my hands were usually red, even when they were no longer frozen.

I soon began to realize that when I toiled with the wires with my concentration totally focused on my work, my hunger pangs would slightly subside. I therefore concealed some wires under my coat and brought them to my bunk. They served a vital purpose, for whenever I was unable to fall asleep due to hunger and cold, I could always distract myself by creating pins.

An elderly German, dressed in civilian clothes, usually observed our work at the factory. On one particular day, he appeared to look in our direction more than usual. I therefore suggested that my sisters keep a steady eye on him and warn me whenever he turned in our direction. This would still provide me with ample time to set aside my pins and do the work I was expected to do. However, though my sisters watched him meticulously, the man, who turned out to be the manager of the factory, appeared to have caught me in the act of private enterprise. I had not been producing what the Nazis had expected of me. Despite the fact that I had been receiving "free food and housing" at the camp, I had not been promoting the German war effort. Although I quickly attempted to set my pins aside and begin to perform my assigned task, it was too late. I was caught in the act, red-handed.

"Don't be afraid," the manager said, as he approached my working table. "I will not harm you in any way. Just show me what you did."

I was totally perplexed. Never had I expected to hear such kind and benign words, expressed with such mildness and mercifulness, from a German. Was I experiencing reality? Was I perhaps dreaming?

I took out all the pins I had created. He looked at my hands and said, "With these little red hands, you can make such pretty things. From now on, you can make your pretty things and I am going to watch you so that the Gestapo will not catch you." I gave him one of my pins and he promised to return to bring me some much-needed food.

He would have loved to bring some milk and bread, but since these foods were rationed and the coupons for these foods allocated to ordinary German civilians did not suffice even for his own family, milk and bread were out of the question. There was a severe food shortage in Germany, and this was the case even in the prewar years, as Hitler's main concern was to build a war machine capable of conquering the world. The starvation of even his own people was of minor concern to him.

The kind gentleman at the Guben factory promised to supply us with fresh vegetables, though, and he fully lived up to his words. For the final two months of our six-month confinement in Guben, we received some much-needed vegetables. I remain fully convinced that this gentleman was surely one of the *chassidei umos ha'olam*, one of the righteous among the nations, who is destined to receive a share in the World to Come (*Tosefta, Sanhedrin* Chapter 13 and *Maimonides, Laws of Repentance*, Chapter 3). Unfortunately, not too many of those saintly individuals were to be found in Nazi Germany any more.

The manager of the Guben factory would often pull up a chair and sit down near my working table to familiarize me with current events. Until these sessions began, I really had no inkling which side was winning the war. We were, of course, all hoping for a quick Allied victory, but at that point, it was nothing more than a mere hope. I was therefore incredibly overjoyed when I was apprised of the fact that the German armies were being crushed and annihilated on all fronts. The Guben factory manager informed me that the noose around Germany was closing ever tighter and tighter. The Russians advancing from the east and the Americans advancing from the west would soon merge in central Germany, and the country would be cut in half. For all practical purposes, Germany had already lost the war. He assured me that our suffering would soon end with the collapse of Nazi Germany.

Unfortunately, however, this assurance had not yet come to fruition and unbearable tortures and persecutions still awaited us. Our ultimate liberation was still not at hand.

ONE MORNING, IN LATE FEBRUARY 1944, WE WERE informed at a morning *appell* that we were leaving Guben. As

Death March usual, our destination was not divulged to us. Many surmised that since the Russian military might was fast approaching the Guben area, it was the intent of the Nazis to move us further away from the rapid Russian advance. When the arrival of Soviet forces became imminent, the evacuations were greatly accelerated. So, too, were the killings. In a labor camp at Brodonica, all Jewish women too sick or too weak to be moved were shot. Similar massacres were reported in many other camps. Only the able-bodied were recruited for the death marches.

In the beginning of 1945, although the German military might was already demolished and the German forces were retreating on all fronts, Hitler had not yet thrown in the towel. He still hoped that the German army would be able to hold out in one of the mountainous areas that remained under his control, either the Sudeten mountains or the Austrian Alps, and from there be able to continue the war.

Thus a new policy now drove the SS to prolong the agony of the death marches. It was their distinct desire to preserve, for as long as possible, a mass of slave labor for all the needs that confronted the disintegrating German army. These laborers would be valuable to the Germans for repairing roads, railway tracks, and bridges, for excavating underground bunkers from which the battles could still be directed, for preparing tank traps to check the Allied advance, and for helping with the massive work involved in preparing mountain fortresses deep underground.

This, then, appeared to be the reason for our sudden and unexpected exit from Guben. We had arrived in Guben at the end of August 1944 and survived a six-month ordeal at the camp. With the German army about to be vanquished and liberation apparently close at hand, no one, even in his wildest imagination, could possibly have envisaged that the worst was yet to come.

Every one of the inmates received one week's supply of bread and margarine, and the march began. We walked in rows of five, escorted on both sides by rifle-bearing soldiers. It was near the end of the winter season, and, with the melting snow sticking to the soles of our wooden shoes, walking became an arduous task. Although we had not been officially informed of our ultimate destination, we appeared to be heading in a northwestern direction, to the German cities of Hamburg and Hanover.

It was a death march in the fullest sense of the term. Whoever chanced to stumble and fall and did not get up quickly to resume the march, whoever found it necessary to rest for several moments, was taken away by horse-drawn carriages and was never heard from again. Other death marches throughout Germany reported similar crimes. In the region of Bechhammer, 1500 Jews were shot while marching.

Alfred Oppenheimer reported at the Eichmann trial that in a march near Gleiwitz, shooting was heard all the time. "We were not permitted to turn our heads," he reported, "but we knew exactly what the shooting meant." All those lagging behind were murdered in cold blood and their bodies thrown into the nearest roadside ditch.

Dr. Aharon Berlin, testifying at the Eichmann trial in 1961, related: [On the march from Birkenau to Kamienna Gora,]

We started counting the shots. It was a long column — 5,000 people. We knew that every shot meant a human life. Sometimes the count reached 500 in a single day. The longer we marched, the more the number of shots increased. There was no strength, no food.

One night, the 4,000 survivors were locked in a long concrete bunker, an air raid shelter. We felt that there was little air in this bunker and the screams, the tragic scenes began — air, air! In the morning, a thousand corpses were found in the bunker, dead of suffocation. People were found in horrible positions, on their knees and with their mouths to the concrete floor. From the pores of the concrete, they had obtained their last breath of air.

On a death march from Auschwitz, some German women, who had heard that we were prisoners, threw boiled potatoes to us. Those who picked up the potatoes died with a bullet — and a hot potato in their mouths.

Not only for the 50,000 from the Auschwitz region, but also for 6,000 or more from the labor camps near Czestochova and other labor camp regions in Central Poland, horrendous westward marches were in progress. One thing is certain: None of those who survived the death marches can ever forget the horror.

At sundown we arrived in a field, where we stopped to rest and eat supper. Supper consisted of boiled potatoes in the skin. We stood in an orderly line as a German soldier passed through those lines, carrying sacks of potatoes. He gently handed several potatoes to each of the inmates.

When the Nazi lieutenant observed this procedure, whereby a member of the master race actually served the lowly creatures in such a refined manner, he ordered him to stop. "Just throw the potatoes to these animals," he screamed with rage.

The soldier attempted to reason with the lieutenant that if the potatoes were thrown, many of the shorter girls would not be able to catch a single potato. His system of distribution assured that each girl received a fair and equal share.

The lieutenant remained unmoved by the soldier's argument and slapped him in the face for his insubordination. The soldier silently moved aside, leaned against a pole, and wept unashamedly. We were all greatly distressed at the cruel treatment accorded to the soldier. Another soldier was then assigned to the task of distributing the potatoes, and the lieutenant's face beamed with pride and joy as the potatoes were "thrown to the animals" as he had ordered. My sisters and I, being too short to join in the potato-catching competition, received none.

We later had an occasion to talk privately with the abused soldier, and he spilled out his story to us. He was born in the Sudetenland in Czechoslovakia, where German was the spoken language. When Germany occupied the Sudeten area after the infamous Munich conference of 1938, the soldier had been extremely proud of his heritage. All of this had changed, he sadly told us. It never dawned on him that Germans could be so cruel and inhumane. The incivility and ferocity of the Nazis cast a dark shadow upon the German Reich. "Germany today, without any ethics and morals, is a jungle, rather than a civilized society," he concluded.

For the night, the Nazis ordered us into silos along the field and then used a padlock to lock each silo from the outside. I was so hungry that I was unable to sleep. I then overheard some girls who had discovered that the Nazis had buried potatoes and turnips in the field. Tiny mounds indicated the exact location of these delicacies, they said. I decided that no matter what the consequences, I simply had to obtain some of these potatoes and turnips. I sprang into action.

During the march, I had picked up a rusty old knife along the road. I now took the knife, made my way to the door, and being extremely thin and small, was able to squeeze my body through the opening underneath the lock. I was now outside the silo. I hoped and prayed that no Nazi would detect my presence outside the silo so I clung tightly to its walls while proceeding to the back of the silo. Had any Nazi apprehended me now, I would have been shot on the spot.

Having reached the back of the silo, I began to run as fast as I could until I discovered the tiny mounds. I proceeded to dig at the first mound I discovered. My rusty knife proved to be a handy implement for this activity. Much to my delight, I suddenly unearthed an abundant supply of potatoes. I picked as many as I could carry underneath my coat and hastily sneaked back to the silo. I had completed my mission successfully and with the help of Hashem, I was still alive.

My older sister and I always consumed our week's supply of bread immediately. I suppose we somehow were determined to find food, no matter what! My younger sister, on the other hand, rationed her bread and always saved for the uncertain morrow.

In the morning following my daring escapade into the potato fields, my younger sister woke up and noticed, much to her dismay, that her leftover bread was nowhere to be found. It had apparently been taken by one of the starving girls in the silo. My sister was heartbroken and shed bitter tears. With great difficulty and with hunger staring her in the face, she had resisted the powerful demands of her stomach and had been able to save her bread and now, she had ended up with nothing. All I could do was to give her some of the raw potatoes I had illegally appropriated during the night. It was all I had. She thankfully consumed these potatoes while tears were still rolling down her face.

During our march, we often met groups marching from other camps. We were all heading in the same direction, although no one was certain as to our ultimate destination. We were, however, well aware of the fact that we were heading toward northwestern Germany. Why were so many Jews marching there? What awaited us when we would finally arrive? These were still mysteries very few attempted to solve.

During supper, when the SS threw the boiled potatoes, the various groups merged to become one large group. Among our new marching partners, we noticed a young girl whose stature and features very much resembled those of our mother. My older sister began talking to her and discovered that she was indeed a relative: a cousin from my mother's side, Barbie Stern from the city of Munkatch. We never really knew about her in the past because her family lived quite a distance from our hometown of Coltova, and communications between various communities in those days was extremely difficult to maintain.

All of us rejoiced with our newly found relative. We hugged and kissed her. We were simply thrilled to begin this new relationship. My older sister extended her open arms and suggested that, from now on, we should always stick together. She even invited her to share our meager supply of food. We would divide our food equally among four rather than among three. She would, in fact, become part of our family.

Although I never expressed my feelings openly, I nevertheless deeply resented my sister's independent course of action. She had consulted no one. Each night, I would somehow consider it to be my responsibility to sneak out of the silo, at the risk of death, to obtain much-needed food supplies for my starving sisters and myself. With so many Nazis patrolling the surroundings, I never knew if I would make it back to the silo alive. The little I managed to bring underneath my coat, though it never satisfied our hunger, helped, at least in a small way, to keep us alive. The thought of having to divide our scarce food supplies among four people, rather than three, annoyed and vexed me and left me with a feeling of deep indignation. This, of course, did not preclude any further nightly escapades on my part. I fully perceived that our situation was critical and that my action was vital for our very survival.

We marched for a period of three weeks, from 7 o'clock in the morning until late afternoon. The Nazis who escorted us traveled mainly in jeeps and on horses. Therefore, they did not share our state of exhaustion. Early each morning, we received some black coffee and before nightfall, boiled potatoes were thrown to us. Silos along the fields marked our humble residences.

Near the end of our march, we reached the outskirts of a large German city. We all presumed it was the Nordic city of Hamburg. During the night, Allied airplanes conducted a ferocious bombing assault on that city. In our quarters, we were able to hear the exploding bombs for many hours, and we enjoyed every moment of it. The bombs were beautiful music to our ears. Though some bombs dropped extremely close to us, none of us was overly concerned about our own safety. We were laughing and we were singing. Despite our ravaged and devastated bodies, our physical condition did not deter us from rejoicing. We had actually witnessed the bombing of one of the major cities of Hitler's Third Reich. The proud Nazis also were vulnerable. What a great feeling this was for us!

Song of the Jewish partisans

One specific song in the Yiddish language was especially popular among the Jewish prisoners. It had reached us from the Jewish partisans who were battling the Nazi hordes in the forests of Europe. The song admonished us that even though dark clouds now hovered over the sunny skies, we must never say that we are traveling on our final journey. The days we have longed and prayed for will eventually arrive, when our thundering drums will clamorously proclaim, "We are here and we are free!" This song instilled much hope within each of us and we sang it with great enthusiasm. Somehow, we felt, we will survive this inferno, the jungle of the "Master Race."

On the day following the Allied bombing, we passed a large metropolis, which we assumed to be Hamburg. Everywhere we looked, we saw ruins and utter destruction. In the areas we passed, hardly a house remained undamaged. The city appeared to be completely covered with rubble and debris.

In some areas in the outskirts of the city, kindhearted German women came outdoors and threw cartons containing milk and bread to us. However, our "gentlemanly" escorts, who marched alongside us with their rifles drawn, shot at any girl who stepped out of line to retrieve the precious goods. Since these items were not thrown directly at us, we were not able to catch them, and we ended up empty-handed. Finally, after three full weeks of constant marching, we arrived in Bergen-Belsen.

When I recently studied the maps of Germany, I concluded without any shadow of doubt, that the city we had passed on our march was not Hamburg. When one travels from Guben to Bergen-Belsen, one does not come anywhere near Hamburg. Hamburg would be completely out of the way. The city we passed could have been either Braunschweig or, more likely, Hanover. Both were large German industrial cities, centers for the manufacture of war supplies, and both were constantly bombed by the Allied air forces. Hanover and Braunschweig are situated on a direct line from Guben to Bergen-Belsen.

BERGEN-BELSEN WAS A NAZI CONCENTRATION CAMP in the vicinity of Hanover. It was established in 1943 as part of

Bergen-Belsen
a prisoner-of-war camp and was intended for Jews whom the German government wished to exchange for Germans imprisoned in Allied territory. Its inmates were Jews possessing passports or citizenship papers of Latin American states, entry visas for Palestine, and others. Between July 1943 and the end of 1944, more than 9,000 Jews from Poland, Greece, Holland, Libya, France, Yugoslavia, and Hungary were transported to Bergen-Belsen.

There was room in the camp for 10,000 inmates, and conditions, though difficult, were at first better than in other camps. However, during 1944, there was a change for the worse. Food rations were reduced to below the minimum nutritional requirement and the prisoners were forced to do hard labor and were cruelly beaten. In addition, whether from malicious intent or due to lack of administrative facilities, the camp authorities failed to provide even the most essential services.

When most of the prisoners had reached the point of physical and spiritual collapse, prisoners who had been

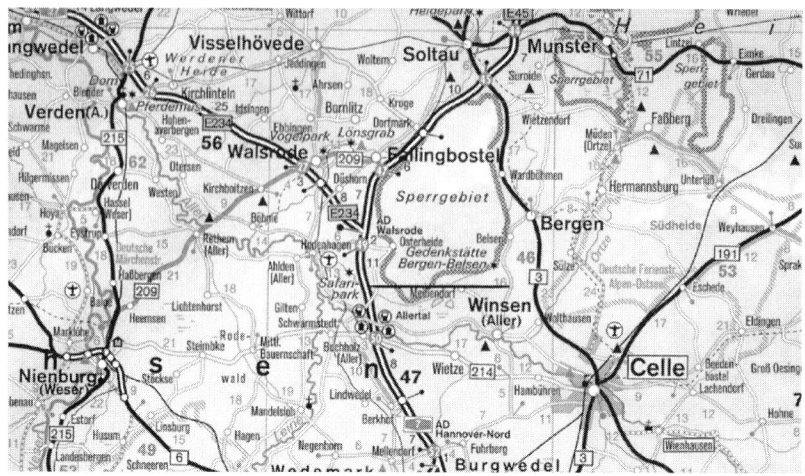

Area near Bergen-Belsen

removed from other camps as a result of the German retreat joined them. The camp population swelled rapidly, from 15,000 in December 1944 to 41,000 in March 1945. The new prisoners, who arrived after forced marches that had sometimes lasted for weeks, were starved and disease ridden. Epidemics broke out, yet there was no medical attention available. The death rate was extremely high. In March 1945, nearly 20,000 people perished. A total of 37,000 died before the liberation.

It was to such prevailing conditions that we arrived at Bergen-Belsen. As we arrived, we were immediately ordered into a large room. We were pushed into such cramped quarters that many girls did not have sufficient space to move. Then the Gestapo locked the doors and windows.

Several minutes later, I developed severe breathing problems. I felt as if I were suffocating. Within moments, I appeared to have become mentally disoriented. A feeling of lightheadedness overcame me and I sensed that I was actually collapsing. Of course, falling down was an impossibility at the time. We were so tightly packed in that room that there was no available space for anyone to fall. Fortunately, someone broke a window and with fresh air now entering the premises, my natural breathing ability was restored and my bodily functions slowly returned to their normal state.

Suddenly, we heard rifle shots emanating from nearby and we all froze with fright and trepidation. The alarm, however, was short-lived, as the shooting soon stopped. We were never able to ascertain who were the victims of this shooting, as we discovered no corpses in the area. Was this shooting simply a Nazi attempt to remind us of our imminent danger? Was this perhaps a warning to us to buckle down and cooperate? Many wondered, but there were no answers.

Shortly thereafter, the Gestapo ordered us into nearby army barracks. So many girls were shoved into the barracks that there was barely enough room to sit. There were certainly no adequate sleeping facilities available. All we could find was some straw on the ground.

Soon, however, we discarded the straw: We threw it all out of our new residential quarters when we discovered that it was swarming with lice. It appeared that Pharaoh's third plague, which had afflicted the Egyptians during our bondage in Egypt, had now invaded Bergen-Belsen in full force. It turned out, unfortunately, that by throwing out the straw, we accomplished very little, as the lice had already settled down in the barracks and were there to stay. In no time at all, the lice were all over our bodies.

Most of the girls in our barracks had arrived before we did and many had already been there for several months. A large group had become infected with typhus, which is a highly contagious disease. Typhus is caused by tiny organisms that look like small bacteria, but often behave like viruses. In humans, they damage the lining and walls of blood vessels, causing bleeding and skin rashes. Some types of these germs infect animals as well as people. Typhus may be transmitted from person to person or from animals to humans by lice, fleas, ticks, or mites. There are several types of typhus, each affecting the human population in different ways.

Epidemic typhus is spread by the human body louse. It has been associated with wars throughout history. Crowding, uncleanness, and human misery during wartime favor the transfer of infected lice from one person to another. Often, more soldiers die of typhus than in combat. The disease was also common, not only in Bergen-Belsen, but also in many other Nazi concentration camps. Scientists estimate that about 25 of every 100 people infected during a typhus epidemic eventually die.

The primary symptoms of typhus are headaches, skin rash, and delirium. It is often recognized by confusion, disordered speech, and hallucinations. The patient's temperature may rise to more than 104 degrees Fahrenheit, remain high for several days, and then drop rapidly. Due to the crowded conditions prevailing in Bergen-Belsen, the unsanitary facilities, and the mass intrusion of the parasitic lice, it is no wonder that typhus was so rampant. A major health epidemic had enveloped the entire camp.

Our food rations at Bergen-Belsen were sparse indeed. For breakfast, we received a piece of black bread, a serving of margarine, and some black coffee. Our supper meal consisted solely of a meager, thin soup, which contained some unknown ingredients. These meals were meant to satisfy our nutritional requirements for the entire day.

After having spent several days in the man-made jungle of Bergen-Belsen, our cousin, Barbie Stern, became gravely ill. She was burning up with an excessively high fever and was inordinately thirsty. I was suddenly overcome by a feeling of guilt, which gave me no rest. My conscience troubled me deeply. "Why did I ever resent her joining us and sharing our meals?" I questioned myself. Now, more than ever, I became convinced that my older sister had chosen the right path when she wholeheartedly invited her to join our group.

I made a valiant effort to assist Barbie. I gave her all my coffee and my tiny piece of margarine. To give up one's coffee in Bergen-Belsen was considered to be a supreme sacrifice, since there was no other liquid available for washing or drinking purposes. The only liquid within our reach was a nearby swamp filled with frogs and overgrown weeds. The water was a greenish color and we had been cautioned to keep away from it for fear that it contained typhus germs. So when I gave up my coffee, the only liquid I consumed for an entire day was the foul water the Nazis chose to call "soup." But I really didn't mind. All of my efforts and concerns were focused toward helping our cousin regain her health.

Barbie, of course, was sincerely grateful for the assistance I was according her and promised to repay me for my kindness when we would again be free. After liberation, she said, she would take me to her sister who resided in Budapest, to use her beautiful bathroom and the shiny bathtub containing warm water. At long last, I would be able to take a bath, clean up, and once and for all get rid of all the lice that were constantly biting my body. She added that she had heard reports that the Budapest Jews were still living at home and had never been transported to concentration camps.

How wonderful these promises sounded! How pleasurable and how delightful it would be to actually bathe in comfort with soap and warm water! By that time, I had scratched my body so intensely to relieve the itch caused by the lice that I was bleeding all over my body. The scratched areas would later become black-and-blue marks.

Despite all my efforts on our cousin's behalf, however, I was unable to save her life. She passed away, yet another victim of typhus. It was a period of deep grief, anguish, and poignant sorrow for us.

It should be pointed out that the report heard by our cousin concerning the deportation of Budapest Jewry only partially agrees with the facts. These are the facts:

In 1941, there were approximately 184,000 Jews residing in Budapest. In July 1944, deportees from Hungary were being taken from the suburbs of Budapest. This news, smuggled out by several escapees, led to demands from the King of Sweden, the Pope, the Geneva-based International Red Cross, as well as from Britain and the United States, to the Hungarian Regent, urging him to halt the deportations. Horty agreed to do so, and the deportations stopped.

By this time, the International Military Tribunal in Nuremberg reported that a total of 437,000 Hungarian Jews had already been deported. More than 170,000 still remained in Budapest. Eichmann had intended to begin the deportations from there early in July.

From Hungary's entry into the war in the summer of 1941 until the German occupation of the country in March 1944, a total of 15,350 members of Budapest's Jewish population perished in labor detachments and through deportation. On November 5, 1944, the Hungarians began handing over Jews to the Germans. Some 76,000 Budapest Jews were involved in the death march and deportations that followed. Of the Jewish inhabitants of Budapest, approximately 105,000 perished between March 1944 and the end of the war.

In Budapest, the Nyilas gangs ruled the streets. On December 28, they entered the Jewish hospital and kidnapped 28 patients. Two days later, all 28 were murdered. On the afternoon of December 31, a gang of 40 to 50 Nyilas broke into the largest of the houses under Swiss protection, the "Glass House" department store, blasting open the locked doors with grenades and opening fire with machine guns. Three Jews were killed. But when the Nyilas tried to attack the 800 Jews in hiding in the building, a Hungarian military unit intervened and the Jews were saved.

To claim that Budapest Jewry was safe from deportations and persecutions simply does not do justice to the historical record of the period. Perhaps the report our cousin heard was merely based *on wishful thinking. We felt so oppressed and our self-image was so downgraded at the time that we actually believed our hopes and dreams to be realities. Our cousin certainly believed that a meeting with her sister was imminent.*

Since, under the circumstances, it was impossible to accord our cousin a decent burial, all I could do was to pull her out to the front of the barracks. With my sisters being so weak and debilitated, it fell upon me to perform this depressing task alone. It was a sickening and truly nauseating scene that greeted me near the front of the barracks. There was a pile of stacked corpses nearly five feet high. I attempted to place our cousin on top of the pile but, alas, my strength and stamina had waned. I had no choice but to leave her at the bottom of the pile.

I then bent down to say my final good-byes. I begged for forgiveness if I had ever hurt or mistreated her during our brief period of acquaintance. With tears in my eyes, I appealed to her that when she entered the Heavenly Court, she should plead with Hashem to have mercy on His people and put an end to this dreadful holocaust that had enveloped us all. "Plead with Him to remove us from darkness to light and from subjugation to redemption," I begged.

I suddenly noticed that our cousin was wearing good leather shoes with laces. Realizing that my cousin no longer had any use for shoes and that I could hardly walk with my wooden shoes, I hesitantly removed her shoes and with my newly found treasure, I sadly returned to the barracks.

Unfortunately, the ever vigilant eyes of the barracks' *Kapo* observed the entire scene. She hastily approached me and demanded the shoes. When I attempted to explain to her the extreme difficulties I endured while wearing the wooden shoes, she was totally unmoved. She slapped my face so hard that I fell helplessly to the ground. Then she viciously ripped the shoes from my feet and left.

Several days later, my older sister Fayge became seriously ill, as she became the next victim of typhus. She was burning up with high fever and could hardly move. My younger sister Golde and I gladly gave our coffee and margarine rations to her.

One night, while we were asleep, a girl sitting directly across from us drank the coffee we were saving for Fayge. When I made that startling discovery in the morning, we were greatly appalled. I sharply reprimanded the girl for her unwarranted act of outright thievery. Rather than deny the charges, the girl began to apologize for what we called her outrageous behavior. She then informed us how sick she had been during the night. She, too, was burning up. Knowing that the coffee was available, she fought valiantly with her conscience to resist her powerful desires to appropriate the coffee for herself. In the end, however, she submitted to her craving.

She sounded so sincere that I truly believed her. There was no false embellishment or exaggeration detectable in her soft voice. I felt truly sorry for her. Unlike us, she was all alone in this world with nobody assisting her in her hour of need. What else could she have done in her critical situation, I thought.

However, Golde, while weeping bitterly, verbally assaulted this girl to no end. "How could you have done such a thing? That coffee was not yours. We were saving it for our sick sister. Do you have any idea how sick she is?"

"Please," I begged my sister, "have compassion for her and leave her alone. That girl is also seriously ill." Golde was so mentally depressed about Fayge's failing health that she had really failed to notice the other girl's acute physical condition. Golde then accepted my advice and offered her wholehearted apologies, which the girl graciously accepted. Sadly, the girl died on the following day, despite our attempts to help her.

Meanwhile Fayge's condition worsened considerably, and she lapsed into a coma. We worked vigorously attempting to revive her, but to no avail. At that time, I became hysterical and lost all hope for our survival. "How can I ever face my parents without my sister?" I cried out loudly. "If my sister dies, I too want to die. It's over. I can't fight anymore! We will surely not survive this jungle!"

Suddenly, a miracle occurred. It was unbelievable. Fayge opened her eyes and began to speak. "Don't lose hope," she said. "Don't you remember that *Tatty* told us never to lose hope?" I will always consider Fayge's awakening a miracle from Hashem, since we knew of no other person who had lapsed into a coma at Bergen-Belsen and eventually recovered. From that day on, Fayge's health began to improve and we hoped and prayed for a complete recovery. My own hopes for survival began a steady upward trend once again. "We can and we will survive with the help of Hashem," I declared.

Having overcome this crisis and the pressures on us having somewhat subsided, my stomach began acting up again and my hunger pangs began creeping to the forefront. "I'm starving and I must obtain some food somewhere," I said to myself. I left the barracks to search for food. It was the beginning of the second week of April, and all the snow had melted. Spring was already in the air. Yet walking with my wooden shoes was most uncomfortable. Because the middle of the sole appeared to be a bit higher than the rest of the shoe, it felt as if snow had become stuck to it. As a result, I wasn't able to walk a straight line and kept swaying back and forth as if I was ine-briated. I felt a whirling sensation in my head. I was very dizzy. When I found an empty tube of toothpaste on the ground, I hastily ripped it apart and began licking the minuscule remain-der of the paste. My, how good that tasted! I was unable to find anything that could even vaguely be referred to as food, though.

During my walk, I chanced upon two girls who had built a small fire. They were mixing flour with water, which they cut into small pieces with a knife and placed into a can of boiling water that was on the fire. They were apparently preparing dumplings. I was utterly amazed at this sight. Where in the world had they obtained the flour and the water? As far as I knew, these edibles were not available for the inmates at Bergen-Belsen. Had they perhaps succeeded in surreptitiously removing these items from the camp kitchen? I stood glued to the spot and could not take my eyes off the tempting food. What would I give for a taste of this delicacy! However, when the girls noticed my presence, they both shouted at me to leave. Perhaps they were concerned that my presence would attract a crowd and amid so many people, their technique for obtaining food surreptitiously would be compromised. I sadly returned to my sisters and with a voice choking with emotion announced my predicament. "I was not able to find any food for us." I felt so helpless at the time. More than ever before, I was now worried about our future. How long could we endure without sufficient nourishment?

That night, I dreamed that I was standing very close to a mountain of dumplings. I began rushing toward that mountain to savor some of its luscious and seductive delicacies, but my feet felt so heavy that I hardly moved. An attempt to reach the dumplings with my hands also proved to be futile. The dumplings were so close, yet not close enough to reach. As I began to cry hysterically, my sisters woke me from this nightmare. It took some time until I was able to compose myself. This was the power of hunger and starvation.

CHAPTER 6
LIBERATION

E HAD SPENT THREE FULL WEEKS IN THE *Gehennom* of Bergen-Belsen when one day we heard loud shouting from the outside. Although my older sister was recovering nicely from her illness, she was still too weak to stand up. My younger sister was also suffering from swollen feet and found it virtually impossible to walk. So it remained for me, alone, to leave the barracks to find out what the commotion was all about.

Much to my delight, I saw British tanks, trucks, and soldiers. Inmates were gathered outside, joyously shouting and cheering. It was April 15, 1945. Our long-dreamed-of day of liberation had arrived!

I hurriedly returned to the barracks in order to share the news with my sisters. Suddenly I began to weep uncontrol-

A British sign near Bergen-Belsen

lably. I was so choked up emotionally that I was unable to utter even a single word. My sisters became greatly alarmed at my unusual and incoherent conduct and anxiously demanded to know what exactly was happening outside. I finally was able to blurt out the words, "The British are here and we are free!" We hugged, and wept with sighs of relief and joy.

When I then closed my eyes to offer a prayer of thanks to Hashem for having delivered us from the Nazi bondage, a vision of my father appeared before me. I imagined seeing my father praying with a *tallis* draped over his head. At that time, I was convinced that he was still alive. He was a physically strong man. Back home, in Coltova, he would have to break through a layer of ice at the *mikveh* before he would be able to immerse himself in its ice-cold waters. Yet, this never deterred him and he never suffered any physical consequences. If we are alive, I reasoned, he too must have surely survived.

Bergen-Belsen was the first concentration camp to be liberated by the Allies, under the command of Field Marshal Viscount Montgomery. Yet even after liberation, the suffering of the inmates had not reached its end. Another 14,000 of the remaining 60,000 died, while the rest were in dire need of medical care. These horrors, which deeply shocked the British soldiers, received widespread publicity in the West. The British arrested the SS administrators, including the commandant, Josef Kramer, and almost all were put to work clearing and burying the 10,000 corpses. Twenty of them died doing this work, probably from infectious diseases. The rest were tried at the end of 1945. Eleven were condemned to death, 19 to imprisonment, and 14 were acquitted.

When the British first entered, Josef Rosensaft later recalled, we — the cowed and emaciated inmates of the camp — did not really believe we were free. It seemed to us a dream, which we feared would turn again into cruel reality.

At Bergen-Belsen, the "cruel reality" came swiftly, as the first British tanks moved on in pursuit of the German forces. For the first 48 hours, the camp remained only nominally under British control, with the Hungarian SS guards remaining in partial command. During that brief interval, 72 Jews and 11 non-Jews were shot by the Hungarians for such offenses as taking potato peels from the kitchen.

Colonel Gerald Draper recalled that men and women, clad in rags, and barely able to move from starvation and typhus, lay in their straw bunks in every state of filth and degradation. The dead and the dying could not be distinguished. Men and women collapsed as they awoke, and fell dead. In order to cope with what they found in verminous and stinking barracks, Draper added, the British army doctors marked a red cross on the foreheads of those they thought had a chance of surviving (*The Nazi Concentration Camps,* pp. 348-49).

Photographs and articles about Bergen-Belsen began to circulate widely in Britain by the end of April, making so great an impact that the word "Belsen" was to become synonymous with inhumanity. These were not reports of discoveries by the Red Army in the distant eastern regions of the Reich, but of horrors seen by men from London and Manchester, from the Midlands and the north of England, battle-weary soldiers familiar enough with the horrors of war by April 1945, but shocked by the sight that confronted them. There had been neither food nor water for five days preceding the British entry. The inmates' clothes were in rags, teeming with lice, and both inside and outside the huts the ground was an almost continuous carpet of dead bodies, human excreta, rags, and filth.

Among the British soldiers who witnessed the first days of liberation at Bergen-Belsen was Peter Coombs, who, in a letter to his wife, described the condition of the survivors:

> *The sight of these (people) affects one profoundly, for while there still is life and movement, we are interested in their salvation both mentally and physically. The conditions in which these people live are appalling. One has to take a tour round and see their faces, their slow staggering gait and feeble movements. The state of their minds is plainly written on their faces, as starvation has reduced their bodies to skeletons. The fact is that all of these were once clean living and sane and certainly not the type to do harm to the Nazis. They are Jews who are dying now at the rate of 300 a day.*
>
> *Every other day, the bodies were collected and buried and there is always an open grave. Ninety-eight British medical students had arrived at Bergen-Belsen to see that the inmates get the right medical attention and food in the right quantities. "It is a living death, an example of Nazi methods, the best indictment of their government one could ever find, and if it is ever necessary, an undoubted answer to those who want to know what we have been fighting for. One feeble movement of the hand in salutation to us from these people is also an answer, for our coming has saved thousands in this camp alone, but for many it is too late"* (Martin Gilbert, *The Holocaust*, pp. 793-96).

Sign near a mass grave at Bergen-Belsen

Although it took three more weeks of British occupation before they were finally able to move us out of the lice-infested barracks, I remain firmly convinced that the British army worked valiantly to improve our miserable lot. They were always courteous and treated us like genuine human beings with utter mercy, charity, and kindness. They did everything for us they possibly could. I, for one, shall always be grateful to the British for going overboard in their efforts to nurse us back to health and to return us to a life of sanity.

The humanitarian efforts of the British soldiers became evident on the very first day of occupation. As soon as the inmates realized that the German authorities had left the camp, many headed straight to the camp kitchen, where large amounts of bread were known to have been stored. However, the British troops prevented them from approaching the premises. Loudspeakers ordered everyone to disperse and return to the barracks. When the starving inmates ignored these orders, the British were forced to use water hoses to repel the large army of inmates on their way to consume the rare and luxurious piece of bread.

Many expressed their utter disappointment in the British soldiers. Was this the liberation we had anticipated for so long? Had the British adopted the Hitler-Himmler policies of persecuting us and starving us to death? We were extremely frustrated and baffled by these British actions.

Soon, however, we discovered that it was solely humanitarian considerations that forced the British to act in this seemingly heartless manner. The Nazis, even with unavoidable defeat staring right at them and with the "Thousand-Year Reich" only days away from unconditional surrender, still had not forsaken their ultimate goal of making the world "Judenrein." Therefore, prior to their departure from the camp, they poisoned all of the remaining bread, thus hoping to murder many additional Jews. Fortunately, the British, in their wisdom, were able to forestall and foil these sinister plans, even at the expense of antagonizing many inmates with their water hoses.

Instead of poisoned bread, the British, on the very first day of occupation, brought thousands of cans containing such essentials as vegetables and other foods into the camp to feed its starving population. The British themselves ate the very same foods.

Having been deprived of such nourishing foods for a long period of time, we felt as if we were eating food items especially prepared for us in Heaven. How delicious and how delightful everything tasted! Naturally, we dug in and ate to our hearts' content. In our preoccupation with consuming these delicacies, we failed to heed the admonition of the renowned Babylonian scholar, Shmuel, that a change in one's regular diet, is the beginning of digestive trouble "שִׁינּוּי וֶסֶת תְּחִילַת חוֹלִי מֵעַיִּים" (*Nedarim* 37b). This was especially true in our situation, when the change to decent and nourishing food occurred so abruptly.

On the following day, we all suffered from diarrhea. There was such an abnormal frequency of intestinal discharge that, in our weak physical state, we were unable to control our bodily functions. It was highly embarrassing to us. Many of the sick and starved girls could not survive such a severe case of diarrhea and, in the coming weeks, died from this ailment.

The Talmud relates that the renowned Talmudic scholar, Rabbi Zadok, fasted and prayed for 40 years in order that Jerusalem might not be destroyed. He became so thin that when he ate anything, the food could be seen as it passed through his throat. When he wanted to restore himself, his disciples would bring him a single fig. He used to suck the juice and cast the rest away. In the tragic year of 70 C.E., when Jerusalem in fact was conquered by the mighty Roman army and the Beis Hamikdash was destroyed, his physical condition was extremely critical. He required immediate medical attention.

Eventually, the renowned Talmudic scholar, Rabban Yochanan ben Zakkai, reached the Roman lines and met with their leader Vespasian. When Vespasian told the rabbi to make requests, which he promised to grant, Rabbi Yochanan requested, "Give me Yavneh and its wise men to be able to organize a Torah seminary, spare me the dynasty of Rabban Gamliel, and send me physicians to heal Rabbi Zadok."

The Roman physicians prescribed that on the first day they let him drink water in which bran had been soaked; on the next day, water in which there had been coarse bran mixed with flour, and on the following day, water that had contained flour (Gittin 56a and b). Recuperation must come gradually, so that the stomach walls can expand little by little.

Obviously, we did not follow the physicians' advice. We jumped into the recuperation full–speed ahead and the result was a massive epidemic of diarrhea.

With my sisters and I all suffering from this dreadful illness, I resolved to leave the barracks to seek outside help. I had absolutely no idea where to turn. I wandered all around the camp, questioned everyone I saw, until one girl informed me that some of the girls had received sacks of rice from the British and they were boiling it for the purpose of feeding the invalids. For many years I had known that rice is recommended as an antidote to diarrhea.

Without any hesitation, I went straight in the direction pointed out to me and I indeed found several girls boiling rice in a large kettle on an open fire.

I begged them to give me some rice for my ailing sisters, but I was turned down. They obviously did not believe my story that my sisters were so sick. I trembled with emotion as I pleaded to them for the rice, as my sisters would surely die if they continued eating the canned foods, but my entreaties were to no avail. As they chased me away, however, they realized that I too had a severe case of diarrhea, and they had a sudden change of heart. They offered me their sincere apologies for having doubted my words, and gave me three portions of rice. From that day on, I went to them every day, and each time they graciously gave me three portions of rice. This kindness was surely a panacea for us in our troubled world at that time.

Meanwhile, right after liberation, a Jewish camp committee was established, headed by Josef Rosensaft from Bedzin, Poland. It actively assisted in the early rescue work, while the Red Cross transported 6,000 sick women to Sweden. The Jewish Relief Unit, representing the Jewish Agency, Anglo-Jewish and American-Jewish organizations, was also active in the camp. There was a struggle with the British authorities to gain permission for Bergen-Belsen to be separately organized as an autonomous Jewish camp, whereas the Allies administered other camps. This was not achieved until May 1946, when the last Polish prisoners left the camp.

Representatives of Jewish communities in the British zone of occupation joined the camp committee, and a central committee for the entire zone was established, also headed by Rosensaft. Thanks to the dedicated efforts of a few women, schools were opened for the 600 children who had survived. A newspaper, *Unsere Stimme*, was eventually established and was widely circulated both in Germany and abroad. Youth movements and Zionist parties opened branches in the camp, and religious life was organized.

After three weeks of British occupation, we were finally moved out of our lice-infested barracks. It was May 6, just one day before Germany surrendered unconditionally. May 6 proved to be a historic day for the Bergen-Belsen inmates. That day will always remain ingrained in my memory. On that day we began to look and feel like humans once again.

FOR THE PREVIOUS SEVERAL WEEKS, ALLIED ARMIES had been closing in on the Germans from all directions.

The Nazis Surrender

Canadian troops under General Crerar had liberated the Netherlands, and Lieutenant General Dempsey's British Second Army headed for Bremen in the north. General Omar Bradley's group of four armies raced eastward to the Elbe River to meet the Russians. In the south, Allied armies under General Devers rolled toward Austria and Czechoslovakia. They hoped to cut off Berlin from the Bavarian mountains, where it was rumored that many determined Germans hoped to make a last-ditch stand.

Late in April, Heinrich Himmler, head of the German home guard and the dreaded Gestapo, tried to negotiate a peace with Great Britain and the United States. The Allies demanded that German troops on all fronts surrender. On April 25, the First Army patrols and Red Army units joined forces at Torgau, on the Elbe River. A few days later, Italian partisans captured and executed Benito Mussolini, who had tried to escape to Switzerland. German forces in Italy surrendered on May 2.

On May 1, German radio announced that Adolf Hitler had died while defending Berlin against the Russians and had named Grand Admiral Karl Doenitz as his successor. Allied investigators later learned that Hitler and his wife, Eva

Braun, had committed suicide in Berlin on April 30 and that their bodies had been burned. Berlin finally fell to the invading Russian armies on May 2.

Early in the morning of May 7, Col. Gen. Alfred Jodl of the German high command entered Allied headquarters in a red school building in Reims, France. There, on behalf of his government, he signed the terms of unconditional surrender. Lt. Gen. Walter B. Smith, General Eisenhower's chief of staff, signed for the Allies. The free world celebrated May 8 as V-E (Victory in Europe) Day. On May 9, a ceremony in Berlin ratified the surrender terms. After five years, eight months, and seven days, the European phase of World War II had ended. The world, at last, was at peace.

On May 6, in the early morning hours, British army trucks pulled up in front of the barracks at the camp. The soldiers placed portable steps near the backs of the trucks and asked us to ascend these steps and enter the trucks. Since my older sister, Fayge, was much too weak to accomplish this task on her own initiative, Golde and I held tightly onto her hands and walked slowly to the truck in order to assist her in her ascent. However, the soldiers immediately noticed Fayge's walking problem. One soldier picked her up and placed her on the truck, and then suggested that I mount the steps on my own and join Fayge inside the truck. This was easier said than done.

As I ascended the first step, my body began to sway in all directions and I was about to fall off the step. The soldier took no chances as he swiftly grabbed me and carried me into the truck. He then did likewise to Golde. We were driven to a section of the Bergen-Belsen camp that housed the bulk of the British soldiers. The purpose of this short journey was to delouse us and provide us with a thorough, and long-awaited, cleaning.

Their first step was to spread a white powder on our entire body and then rub it into our hair, apparently to destroy the lice, which were lodged within our bodies. When we were then escorted to the showers, chaos erupted. Some girls were too

Alfred Jodl signs the unconditional surrender terms of German forces. He was eventually executed for his war crimes.

fearful of entering the showers. We had all heard reports from other concentration camps that when inmates were taken to the showers via doorways clearly marked with the word *"Brause"* (the German word for shower), they soon discovered, much to their dismay, that it was not water that flowed from the pipes, but rather, poison gas. Despite the fact that civilized human beings were now in complete charge of these chambers, some girls were still quite hysterical. They were possessed by an unmanageable fear and emotional excess. They displayed an understandable emotional panic, simply refusing to enter the shower chambers.

In the end, the supervising German women were very persuasive. With their calm and serene deportment, they were able to convince the girls that there was absolutely no danger involved. On the contrary, the showers were designed solely for the welfare of the inmates. It was a step in the direction of improved health.

After the showers, the women distributed new sets of clean clothing, free from contamination and disease, to everyone. I received a dress, a spring coat, and a pair of shoes. We received no undergarments, as, I assume, the British had none at their disposal. The clothes we received were all secondhand, but they felt clean and comfortable. In addition, each inmate received a brand-new towel, which I immediately wrapped around my neck. Since it was early May and the temperature was quite moderate, I could not comprehend why I always felt cold and chilly. The towel thus proved to be extremely handy for me. The women then escorted us to clean army barracks and we were assigned bunk beds. These were our first decent sleeping quarters since we left Coltova almost a year earlier.

These German women acted toward us with the utmost dignity and respect. They were courteous, friendly, and kind, and treated us as bona fide human beings. Unlike the British soldiers, who spoke only English, these women, who spoke German, were easily able to converse with me and with the Yiddish-speaking inmates. Thus, they were able to share with us many of the current events in the outside world.

I have often wondered about these women's real feelings toward our people. Either they had never supported the Nazi agenda and vehemently disapproved of Hitler's uncivilized methods, or perhaps they were listed among Hitler's passionate supporters and had a change of heart only when the victorious Allied armies conquered their hometowns. They may have realized that it is always a wiser policy to stick with the victor. We shall never know the answer to this question.

For the first supper in our new barracks we were served chicken soup and chicken. We were overjoyed to be able to eat good, nourishing food. It tasted so delicious! Compared to the food we had been eating for almost a year, this meal could truly be classified as a banquet. Unfortunately, however, when I finished the soup, I was so fully satiated that I found it difficult to eat the chicken. My stomach walls, apparently, had not yet expanded sufficiently to allow me to partake of all the food my heart desired.

Since the lavish chicken banquet turned out to be only a one-time occasion, we had no alternative but to return to the canned food. Unfortunately, however, the plague of diarrhea was persistent and returned in ever increasing severity. We appeared to be on the verge of starvation once again. I, therefore, began to seek other means to supplement our nutritional requirements.

I decided to walk to the nearby village to try my hand at begging. Although my parents had taught me that begging was not the most honorable profession, I nevertheless felt that begging to save the lives of human beings was both virtuous and proper. I entered a German home, and related our horrendous experiences to the lady of the house. I then pleaded with her and beseeched her to give me some milk and bread to save the lives of my starving sisters. The kind woman graciously complied with my request and gave me as much food as I could possibly carry in my hands. Since I didn't have a basket or even a simple box at my disposal, all I was able to carry back was one carton of milk and one thick piece of bread. Upon my return to the camp, I discovered that other girls had made similar excursions to the nearby village, and virtually all of their efforts had been crowned with success.

On the following day, I decided to try the art of begging once again. I met yet another kind lady who generously gave me milk, bread, and some fresh vegetables. However, before leaving her house, she opened her heart to me and expressed her deep fears and anxieties. She related that people from the camp had been entering her private property for the past several days without any authorization whatsoever, and helping themselves to anything they desired. They had been purloining live chickens, garden vegetables, and fruits off the trees. Her neighbors had even complained that sometimes these young men actually had broken into their homes to plunder and to loot even articles of clothing. The village residents had been powerless to prevent these gross violations of civil law.

The woman then added that she was well aware of the persecutions and tortures perpetrated upon these people. Just a brief glance at their faces clearly pointed to the deprivations they had suffered. "But what do these people want from us?" she asked me. "We are poor and humble civilians, barely earning a livelihood. If our fruits and vegetables will be pillaged, what will we eat?" She concluded her remarks by adding that she knew of no one in that village who ever supported the tyrannical acts of the Nazis. Many were not even aware of them. I left the woman's home with a feeling of deep compassion for her plight.

On my way to the village the following day, a young man, an inmate of our camp, approached me and inquired in a rather harsh tone about my destination. When I responded to his inquiry and also informed him of the purpose of the trip, he thundered at me with much anger and rage, "Do you mean to tell me that you go to the Germans to beg for bread? After they robbed us of all of our property and killed our families, you still go begging to them? Have you no shame? From the Germans," he thunderously proclaimed, "you do not beg. You take! Because of what they did to us, they owe us everything we take and even much more!"

I attempted to explain to him that I no longer had the strength to fight the Germans, to take their property and run. My main concern at present was the health and welfare of my sisters. I did not want them to die, now that we had survived the German camps.

The man suggested that I go with him. He promised to supply me not only with bread, but also with freshly cooked chickens and clean clothing. "Why should a beautiful girl, possessing such sparkling eyes, be subjected to wearing such filthy rags?" he asked.

When he wondered why I was wearing a towel around my neck in the warm days of June, I told him that I had probably contracted a sickness because I always felt so cold and chilly. Despite his tempting and magnanimous offers, I chose not to follow this man. I didn't know who he was and I was intuitively afraid of him. Instead, I performed what had by now become a daily routine chore. I solicited food at the home of another German family and was rewarded with milk, bread, two cucumbers, and several scallions.

Early the next morning, when I left the barracks to tend to my daily business at the village, a British soldier greeted me by saying, "Good morning," in a very friendly manner. I was so startled that an apparently decent and civil human being, a member of the British armed forces, would greet me in such a friendly and amicable fashion, that for the first time in more than a year, I really saw myself. I suddenly noticed my dirtiness, my extreme slovenliness, and my utter neglect. I was so embarrassed and so ashamed. My appearance resembled that of a hag. Rather than proceeding to the village as I had planned, I returned to the barracks and wept uncontrollably.

My sisters were terrified when they noticed my strange and unusual behavior, and demanded to know its cause. Why was I so depressed? What had occurred outside the barracks? "I am so filthy," I sobbed, "that I feel ashamed to go out like this again."

I was so emotionally vulnerable that my sisters felt that it would be best for me to go to bed immediately. Rest and sleep were the order of the day. Then, in spite of the fact that both of them could hardly walk, they struggled to the bathroom to wash my clothes.

The next day, I resumed my trip to the village and succeeded in obtaining the usual milk and bread plus several vegetables. On the way back to the camp, I was unexpectedly accosted by British troops, who then confiscated all of the food I had in my possession. I was heartbroken and overcome with sorrow. I had debased myself by begging like a cheap and lowly creature, all for the purpose of feeding my sisters, and now I was returning to them empty-handed. I wondered if the British had adopted some of the Nazi tactics of depriving innocent civilians of their physical needs. After all, these products had been acquired legally, without any coercion whatsoever. Was this the liberation we had prayed and hoped for?

I began to plead with the soldiers to return the food they had confiscated, but, unfortunately, I did not succeed. A language barrier stood between us and, as a result, it was often difficult for us to communicate with them. Since I spoke to them in German, they simply could not comprehend what I was saying. Likewise, I was unable to understand their English. Therefore, though we spoke to each other, we actually made no contact with each other. The soldiers returned me to the barracks, together with many other girls they had seized at the village.

Before they actually released us, a German-speaking soldier announced over the microphone that the German villagers had complained to the general that *Haeftlinge* from the Bergen-Belsen camp were invading their village daily and plundering and pillaging to their hearts' content. Therefore, it had been decided that, from that moment, no one would be permitted to go to the village. If someone violated this directive for the purpose of obtaining food and other goods, the authorities would be compelled to confiscate those items. In addition, the announcement concluded, there would be more serious consequences for violations of the rules.

Although, at the time, I deeply resented the callousness of the British authorities and I strongly felt that they should have demonstrated greater consideration and displayed more understanding because of the plight of the *Haeftlinge,* now, in retrospect, I realize that the actions of the authorities were justified both ethically and morally. It is imperative that a conquering army treat all civilians in the conquered nation as innocent neutrals. Vengeance toward former enemies will only lead to chaos and utter confusion. The conqueror must maintain law and order to assure the safety and security of all citizens. Domestic tranquility must prevail at all times. To allow the camp inmates unlimited access to the village, where they would feel free to mete out their own measure of justice, would be totally unacceptable among civilized nations. Only the Nazis and their like resorted to such methods. Thus, I now strongly feel that the actions taken by the British during their occupation of the Bergen-Belsen camp were totally fitting and proper.

When I returned to our barracks after my temporary arrest, I threw myself onto the bed and informed my sisters of the latest developments. I concluded with the words, "I'm exhausted and I feel sick."

At first I felt extremely cold, and then I felt extremely hot. Eventually, I lapsed into a state of delirium. I imagined I saw my mother. Her face was dark and covered with many blackheads. This greatly perturbed me, as my mother's skin had always been so white and soft. I remember telling her, "Mommy, I'm so sick!" When my sisters overheard me mumbling to myself and realized that I had become delirious, they rushed to call the nurse who had been assigned to the barracks. She in turn summoned an ambulance, which drove me to a provisional hospital that had been constructed in the style of the barracks, and which catered especially to the needs of Holocaust survivors.

Before a room was assigned to me, I was given a sponge bath by a German woman. I was delighted to be serviced by the Germans for a change, as up to that point, I had been forcibly servicing them. The woman appeared to be extremely sad and downcast. She just performed her duties and didn't utter a single word to me. Since the British had specifically singled out former German camp supervisors and forced them to clean up the mess they had created at the camp and also made them bury the many corpses they had left unattended, many felt that these German women, the former camp guards, were specifically enlisted to ameliorate the health crisis by catering to sick inmates. I can well imagine how abused and how downtrodden these women must have felt when they, possessing "master race" credentials, were forced to perform menial work for lower-class creatures like Jews.

After I was assigned to a room, it was time for supper. I was served boiled chicken with mashed potatoes. How heavenly that tasted! Being once again unable to consume the canned foods because of the diarrhea potential, I had reached the point of starvation before this meal helped to reinvigorate me.

After supper, a German nurse weighed me. I was shocked to discover that I weighed no more than 25 kilos, the metric equivalent of about 55 pounds. A physician then X-rayed me and gave me a complete physical examination. Anxiously, I waited for his diagnosis. It was not a happy one: The doctor concluded that I was suffering from both pneumonia and tuberculosis.

I asked the doctor, "Did I survive the hell of Nazism just to die now?"

I had always known that tuberculosis was an incurable disease. The doctor assured me that I would live a long life. My prognosis was good. The doctors would help me and I would get well. I must say that I did not believe the doctor's rosy, optimistic assurance for even a moment. I was convinced that I was nearing the end of my life. The doctor was merely attempting to cheer me up and lift my spirits, I thought.

The doctor then informed me that although I might not have been aware of it at the time, all the black-and-blue marks all over my body clearly indicated to him that I had, at one time, contracted the black typhus disease. When I explained to him that these marks were the results of constant scratching on my part due to the biting lice that had infested my body, he refused to accept my explanation and insisted that scratching alone could not have produced so many huge blotches on my skin.

On the other hand, I had seen many inmates at the camp that had contracted the black typhus. They generally were plagued with extremely high fever. They were bedridden and could barely move around. I had no such symptoms. Perhaps I merely had only a slight case of typhus, which could have contributed, at least partially, to my body blemishes.

CHAPTER 7
RECOVERY IN SWEDEN

S I WAS SLOWLY BEGINNING MY ARDUOUS recovery, a social worker visited my sisters and asked about their future plans when they left Bergen-Belsen. When my sisters told her that they had every intention of returning home to Coltova, the social worker advised them not to return home just yet. She explained to my sisters that I was seriously ill, that I required much medical care, and that without sufficient funds, I would not be able to receive the necessary medical attention so essential for my complete recuperation. She then informed us that the Swedish government, headed by King Gustavus, had generously offered to take care of all sick people who survived the concentration camps. In Sweden, these victims of the Holocaust would be provided not only with all of their physical needs, but Sweden would also open all of its medical facilities and

126 ☐ HOPE NEVER DIES

provide the best medical attention possible. The social worker strongly urged us to avail ourselves of this opportunity. She promised that all three of us could go together. The Red Cross and the United Nations Relief and Rehabilitation Administration (UNRRA) would be instrumental in transferring us to Sweden.

The aftermath of National Socialism's victory in Germany in 1933 had created a Jewish refugee problem in Sweden. Efforts by Swedish Jewish refugee organizations to save German Jews by transferring them to Sweden were impeded by the country's restrained refugee policy. The authorities feared that the refugees would increase the unemployment from which Sweden had suffered badly as a result of the 1929 world crisis, and that anti-Semitism would grow because of an increasing Jewish population. The upper echelon of Swedish society had been pro-German even from earlier years.

During the Second World War however, public opinion changed in favor of the refugees for several reasons. The crimes of the Nazis, which many circles had previously refused to admit, became publicly known. After the war, instead of unemployment, there now was a shortage of workers. Moreover, it was realized that, with some good will, it would be possible to receive many more refugees than was previously thought.

The turning point in the history of the Swedish refugee policy and anti-Semitism came in November 1942, when Jewish persecutions in German-occupied Norway began. This provoked a general feeling of disgust, and angry protests were expressed throughout Sweden. Approximately 900 Norwegian Jews who were able to escape to Sweden were readily accepted.

How decisive the change of mind was in Sweden became obvious in October 1943, when Danish Jewry took flight in order to escape deportation. After a fruitless diplomatic discussion with the German foreign office, the Swedish government officially offered asylum to the fleeing Jews, setting an example of humane policy. Encouraged by the turning tide of the war, the unanimous public opinion in Sweden, and the acclaim of the free world, the Swedish government received not only about 8,000 Jews from Denmark, but also an almost equal number of Danes fleeing from the German occupation. Moreover, it tolerated the establishment of a clandestine organization on its soil, providing the Danish resistance movement with steadfast communication with the Allies. The communication lines were initiated and maintained with the organizational and financial aid of the Swedish and Danish Jews.

Some leaders of the Jewish community in Stockholm were also instrumental in bringing about the mission of Raoul Wallenberg to Hungary in 1944, where he became one of the main benefactors and rescuers of the Budapest Jewish community. Under the guidance of the World Jewish Congress (WJC), toward the end of the war, Sweden became an important center for the dispatch of food parcels to concentration camp inmates, mainly in Germany. Finally, the ties formed by the WJC representative with Himmler's masseur led to the historic meeting of Norbert Mazur with Himmler on the eve of Germany's final defeat. Following their negotiations, many more thousands of concentration camp inmates were included in the rescue operation of Count Folke Bernadotte.

Thus, Sweden's generous, magnanimous offer to open its gates to all the diseased victims of the Holocaust was only a continuation of a well-trodden path, a path filled with compassion and mercy. The Swedes completely lived up to their word and nurtured many individuals back to good health. Their humanitarian gestures probably saved my life. I entered Sweden seriously ill and with the help of Hashem, I left there in good health. I certainly owe the Swedes my lifelong thanks and gratitude.

When my sisters discussed our potential trip with me, I despaired. How would we succeed in finding the rest of our family if we went to Sweden? My older sister assured me that we would be able to search from there. In fact, the Swedes had volunteered to assist in this search. In addition, my sister continued, the fresh Swedish mountain air would do wonders for us and help in our recovery. Having been reassured and with my confidence restored, I agreed to go.

It often seems that few things ever go smoothly and often, complications arise. This time, the social worker visited me in the hospital to discuss our travel arrangements. She informed me that my sisters would be sailing for Sweden, whereas I would have to remain a while longer. "Your health does not permit you to travel immediately. You are not quite ready yet," she said.

"I am ready!" I shouted at the top of my voice, "and I'm feeling fine." I added that the Germans had been unable to separate us and they, too, would not separate us.

The woman responded, "We have no intentions of separating you. In one week, you too, will be able to leave Germany and you'll all meet in Sweden."

However, I adamantly insisted that we either go together or we would not go at all. As the social worker was leaving, she remarked that she was really hopeful that I would change my mind. "We are completely on your side," she concluded, "and we truly wish to help you."

When my sisters came to visit me in the hospital that day, they found me silently weeping. "You are not going to leave without me, are you?" I asked.

My older sister responded gently and blandly. "Even though the social worker has assured us that in a very short time, we would be reunited in Sweden, we will, of course, not sail for Sweden if you insist that we remain with you. The only reason you are to remain in Germany a while longer is that the ship on which you are scheduled to sail is not equipped to accommodate sick people." She concluded by assuring me, "These people are not Nazis. Our welfare is their sole concern and we can safely place our full trust in them." I finally consented that they leave the cursed earth of Germany without me, and they left several days later.

A little more than a week passed before I finally left the hospital. An ambulance drove some other sick girls and me to the port city of Luebeck, which lies on the Trave River near the Baltic Sea. There, we waited for several hours before a ship arrived to take us to Sweden. During our wait, we were provided with cornflakes and bananas. I ate so many bananas on that day that an upset stomach was the inevitable result. For many years thereafter, I became nauseated whenever I merely looked at a banana.

The ship finally arrived. It was an ambulance ship, fully equipped medically. Each one of the girls was provided with her own private nurse. Even though they were Swedish nurses, they all spoke German fluently and I was able to communicate with them easily. Several hours after we boarded, the ship docked in Stockholm, the capital of Sweden.

With several hours to spare, before we resumed on the next leg of our journey, my private nurse rented a car and took me on a two-hour tour of the city of Stockhom, which became Sweden's capital in the 17th century. In 1953, it celebrated its 700th anniversary. It is truly a beautiful city. It lies on a dozen islands and along the shores of Lake Malar, where the lake meets the Baltic Sea on Sweden's eastern coast. Over a thousand small islands lie on the Saltsjon Bay of the Baltic Sea outside Stockholm. The city is called the "Venice of the North" because of its location and many waterways. The sparkling cleanliness of the streets and buildings, the magnificence of its old palaces, and the sharp clean lines of its office buildings make the city an expression of Swedish character.

The vast Djurgarden Park has been a pleasure resort of the people of Stockholm since the 17th century. The park contains a zoo and a large open-air museum. The buildings of the museum represent different historical periods. The Stockholm Town

Thousands of boats sail along Sweden's coasts and inland waterways

Hall, completed in 1923, with its three golden crowns, is one of the finest buildings in Sweden. Many other historic buildings are distinguished for their beauty. On a small island stand the Riksdag, or parliament building, and the Riksbank, the oldest government-owned bank in the world.

I enjoyed the tour tremendously, not only because I was able to take my mind off my own real problems, and focus on the more pleasant aspects of life, but also mainly because of the exceptional kindness and generosity displayed by the Swedish nurse. She was magnanimous at all times, showing nobility of feeling and generosity of mind. I was now fully convinced that my journey to Sweden was a giant step in the right direction. In this country, I could, with the help of Hashem, be fully nursed back to normal health. Swedish citizens actually considered us to be genuine human beings.

We boarded a ship again and our destination this time was Goteborg, Sweden's second largest city. Goteborg lies on the Kattegat. The Goete Canal connects it with Stockholm, 150 miles to the northeast. It is on this very canal that we sailed from Stockholm to Goteborg. From there, we were driven by ambulance to the summer resort of Ramlosa Brun, which had been converted for us, the Holocaust survivors, into a hospital. Here, our road to recovery would commence.

As soon as I arrived in Ramlosa Brun, my older sister telephoned. She informed me that she was recovering nicely in a convalescent home. She and my younger sister had been given a thorough examination by a physician, who diagnosed my younger sister's ailment as tuberculosis. She was now confined to a local hospital, but would soon be transferred to Ramlosa Brun, where we would both be united once again.

She also informed me that although she did not know her exact address, she had written to our mother's younger sister, our Aunt Chanah, in the United States. The letter was addressed to Chanah Roth, Gary, Indiana, U.S. Much to her surprise, the letter arrived and Aunt Chanah immediately telegraphed to us $10, which was a considerable amount at the time. Our joy was immeasurable, as we had found at least one living and close relative somewhere on earth.

To date, we had not received any information concerning our parents, four brothers, and one other sister. Had they survived? Were they still alive? Where might they be? These and many other similar questions raced through our minds and gave us no rest. We pondered these questions constantly.

Having discovered her address, I, too wrote to Aunt Chanah and from then on, each of her return letters included a $10 bill, which I gladly shared with my younger sisters. It was all that we owned at the time. We had no other material possessions.

Aunt Chanah had immigrated to the United States in 1931. Her husband, Uncle Chaim Ber, had preceded her by two years. He settled in Gary, where many of his relatives resided. When, as the proprietor of a grocery store, he felt financially secure, he sent for his wife and two sons. In the United States, they were blessed with a daughter. Uncle Chaim Ber and Aunt Chanah were to play a prominent role in once again reconstructing for us a normal and civilized life.

When I first arrived in Ramlosa Brun, I felt that I was extremely corpulent and obese. However, when a physician weighed me, my total weight was a mere 30 kilograms, a little over 66 pounds. I was literally amazed. "How could I appear to be so excessively fat when I only weighed 30 kilograms?" I questioned the doctor. Back home in Tornalya, I weighed 32 kilograms (about 70.5 pounds) and I appeared quite slender. This conundrum puzzled me greatly. The doctor assured me that I was, in reality, not overweight at all. My body was distended and inflated to these unreasonable proportions as a result of excessive eating after a long period of starvation. This was a natural phenomenon under my circumstances, he assured me.

As a matter of fact, I did consume too much food. I always felt hungry. I often would wrap potato peels in my napkin and later eat them in seclusion. I was really ashamed of my eating so excessively, but I seemed to be unable to curb my physical appetite. I craved food, for I had promised myself never to be hungry again. Of the five girls rooming with me at Ramlosa Brun, one constantly teased me with regard to my obesity and although I felt both harassed and annoyed, I exerted virtually no effort to alter my habits in this area.

One day, we were informed that an eminent Swedish dignitary would be visiting Ramlosa Brun. We were pleasantly surprised to discover that the distinguished visitor would be a member of the royal family, none other than the Crown Princess Louise, wife of Gustavus VI, who would eventually sit on the Swedish throne. Princess Louise herself was descended from royalty, as she was a close relative of Lord Earl Mountbatten, who was the son of Prince Louis Alexander, a cousin of King George V of England. The purpose of her visit was to raise our spirits and help us regain the confidence and self-reliance many of us seemed to have forfeited in the jungles of Nazism. Her visit would also help to assure us of the sincere desire of the Swedish people to treat us with utmost

Crown Princess Louise of Sweden

dignity and esteem, and to tell us that we were most welcome in her country.

The princess completed her mission most admirably. She remained in our room for almost 30 minutes, and her friendship and love toward us was magnificently displayed in her very eyes. How they sparkled with joy! She chatted with us, she laughed with us, and she showed us so much love. It almost felt as if she were an ordinary commoner.

Before she left, I presented her with a reindeer, which I had created from thin wires as I had done in the camps. She graciously thanked me and gave me a bunch of grapes. Her visit was one that shall always be ingrained in my mind.

After having spent several days at Ramlosa Brun, I suffered an unexpected relapse, as my pneumonia returned. In addition, I now had fluid in my lungs, and the doctors redefined my condition as more serious. They began to check me more thoroughly. I was constantly X-rayed, while the fluid was extracted from my lungs. Since these functions were performed in a different building of the hospital complex, male nurses transported me there on a stretcher. Like the other Swedes, they were very kind and treated us with the utmost dignity and respect.

One day, a male nurse, who had been wheeling me to the other building to be X-rayed, began to converse with me. Although he spoke in a broken German, I was clearly able to comprehend his words. He had recently been reading detailed reports of the tortures and persecutions we had endured at the concentration camps and told me that he truly felt our sorrow and anguish. He would love to be of assistance in any way possible. "Civilization has let you down," he said, "and it is now my intent to upgrade and alleviate your tragic situation." He asked what could he do for me.

The man appeared kind, generous, and goodhearted. Therefore, I suggested that perhaps he could bring me some bread. In spite of the fact that the Swedes provided us with nutritious meals, and adequate amounts of it, my hunger was not completely satisfied. As sick as I was, my appetite never decreased. There was always an inherent craving for more food. The man kept his word and on the following day, he presented me with a large loaf of bread.

WHEN ON THE NEXT DAY THE MALE NURSE LEFT A *krone* (a monetary unit used in Sweden, and, at the time,

New Friends

valued at approximately 20¢) on my bed, I felt greatly embarrassed. How could I, a religious girl, accept money from strange men? Did the man perhaps have ulterior motives? What could this lead to? Yet despite my discomfiture, I felt too shy and diffident to return the coin.

My roommate, Kitty W. who originally came from the Slovakian town of Kosice (Kaschau), immediately noticed my predicament and inquired whether I would like to return the coin. When, after a brief delay, I finally replied in the affirmative, it was too late. The man had already left the room. Kitty, however, was unperturbed and unabashed. She hastened to the window, where the man was just passing by, threw the *krone* down to him and loudly exclaimed, "Serena [my Hungarian name] does not want your money." I was greatly agitated at Kitty's abrupt and impetuous action. This certainly was not my style. However, henceforth, the matter remained a closed book.

Kitty's younger sister, Suzie, also shared our room. Both had been raised in a secular Jewish home and had

My friend Suzie W.

virtually no knowledge of Jewish history, its culture, and its religion. Their roots, their origin, and their background were complete mysteries to them. They had grown up in a home totally devoid of any Jewish content, a home denuded of Judaism's traditional symbols and unique life patterns, with the result that it differed only slightly from the non-Jewish home. The Jewish way of life had been whittled down and had taken on the protective coloration of the general environment.

Now Suzie had become my roommate and was confronted with a completely different lifestyle. Since I had been raised in a traditional Jewish home, where Torah and Judaism pervaded the very atmosphere, where Jewish education played such a prominent and most vital role, it was only natural for Suzie to become captivated by the traditions she now observed. She noticed everything with her eyes wide open and she learned.

She observed my daily prayers, she observed my washing before meals and the subsequent pronouncements of the appropriate blessings, she observed the recitation of *Birkas Hamazon* (Grace After Meals), she observed the *K'rias Shema*, always said before retiring, and the special prayers said upon rising in the morning, and she observed that lights were not turned on or off on Shabbos. Suzie became quite enthusiastic about the Jewish religion and was anxious to discover more of its gems.

Once, when Suzie was about to turn on the lights on Shabbos, she looked at me and proudly proclaimed, "If Serena does not turn on the lights on Shabbos, neither will I!" She then approached me and asked me to teach her to pray. Since I had a *siddur* in my possession, I began teaching her the *alef-beis*. She was 17 years old and learned quickly. After she had successfully mastered the Hebrew-reading skills, I began teaching her the prayers. Suzie was now well on her way to observing authentic Judaism.

I then began an earnest dialogue with Suzie. I listened to her questions carefully and certainly did not reject her simply because her questions may have challenged my prior assumptions and beliefs. I talked to her both patiently and placidly, about her roots, her origin, her background, and her identity. Dialogue is a prerequisite for sound teaching. The Torah enjoins us (*Devarim* 6:7): "You shall teach them thoroughly to thy children and you shall speak of them" — "וְשִׁנַּנְתָּם לְבָנֶיךָ וְדִבַּרְתָּ בָּם."

When the renowned Lubliner Rav, Harav Meir Shapiro, was questioned as to which methods and techniques he would employ in dealing with an alienated child or with one who had never been exposed to a life of Torah, he referred the questioner to the Book of Melachim II, Chapter 4. He suggested that the methods employed by the prophet Elisha would be most effective.

Upon perusing the chapter, one finds that it deals with a barren Shunamite woman, who for many years longed for a child. Elisha prophesied that her prayers would indeed be answered and ultimately, she gave birth to a son. Tragedy, however, struck soon thereafter, and the child died. From Biblical accounts, one notes two attempts to revive the child. At first, Gechazi, Elisha's assistant, rushed to the youngster and placed his staff upon him, but to no avail. Finally Elisha arrived on the scene. "He lay upon the boy, placing his mouth upon his mouth, his eyes upon his eyes, and his palms upon his palms. He stretched himself out *over him and warmed the flesh of the boy." (Melachim II 4:34).*

"וַיַּעַל וַיִּשְׁכַּב עַל הַיֶּלֶד וַיָּשֶׂם פִּיו עַל פִּיו וְעֵינָיו עַל עֵינָיו וְכַפָּיו עַל כַּפָּיו וַיִּגְהַר עָלָיו וַיָּחָם בְּשַׂר הַיָּלֶד."

When a child rebels and opts to leave the tradition of his ancestors, when he becomes alienated from his faith and dies a spiritual death, or when he has never entered the chambers of holiness and had never been taught the basics of our faith, then Gechazi's method, interpreted the Lubliner Rav, is doomed to certain failure. "Placing the stick upon the child," striking him, rejecting him, and shocking him into revival will not work with the contemporary child. Such tactics are often counterproductive and have adverse effects. They tend to drive the child even closer into the embracing arms of alien cultures and ideologies.

What method did Elisha propose? "Place your palms upon his palms." Take the child by the hand and lead him out of his confused state of mind. "Place your eyes upon his eyes." Look him straight in the eye. Convince him of the wholeheartedness of your convictions and of the sincerity of your motives. It is imperative for the child to detect in his mentor the honest and sincere hero image. The child must be convinced that the mentor is in earnest and is himself permeated by the holiness, sublimity, and truth of his words. Finally, "place your mouth upon his mouth." Begin a dialogue with the child.

The results will be most gratifying. "The flesh of the child will become warm." The child, who initially was cold and unresponsive, who was obtuse and unreceptive to the principles of our faith, or one who was never exposed to a life of Torah, will gradually begin to respond. He will manifest a more profound interest in the cherished values and beliefs of Judaism. He will inquire with more intensity, he will question with greater fervor and passion. The questioning will then turn into a quest, into a yearning, into a thirst to drink from the rich fountains of our tradition.

I attempted to use these very methods and techniques proposed by the Lubliner Rav in conveying to Suzie the basics of our faith. They seemed, at least for the time being, to have had some measure of success, as Suzie appeared to discover her true identity as a Jew. I am eternally grateful to Hashem for having helped me in this endeavor.

Shortly thereafter, Suzie became very sick. She had contracted a severe case of pneumonia. With Yom Kippur soon approaching, Suzie

R' Meir Shapiro, the Lubliner Rav

was determined to fast the entire day. The nurses beseeched and implored her to take her regularly prescribed medication and drink some water, but to no avail. She remained adamant and inflexible. She prayed and fasted all day. Miraculously, the fast did not impair her physical condition. Several days after Yom Kippur, her temperature was normal once again and she soon recovered, not only from pneumonia but also from a touch of tuberculosis.

Due to her marvelously speedy recovery, Suzie was soon discharged from the hospital. Since her American relatives had long ago sent her an affidavit, the American consulate was able to issue her a visa and she immigrated to the United States to begin a new life. Of course, we corresponded with each other. Our common ordeal at Ramlosa Brun had created a close and warm bond of friendship between us and we were determined not to permit the Atlantic Ocean to sunder us apart.

After a short while, I received a most shocking letter from her. The letter struck me with surprise and horror. Suzie informed me that her American relatives were secular Jews and not religious at all. As a result, though she had already been residing in New York for several weeks, she had yet to meet her first religious Jew. However, in this secular environment, she had been introduced to a nice and decent Italian boy, and she planned to marry him.

What had happened to Suzie in a period of just weeks in the United States? Could an environment so dominate and so influence well-intentioned people? I felt betrayed, devastated, and ravaged by this unexpected turn of events. In spite of everything she had learned about *Yiddishkeit*, we ended up losing her. She had become just another victimized soul in the jungle of secularism.

I was then reminded of our Talmudic sages, who taught long ago, "Woe to the wicked and woe to his neighbor" — "אוֹי לְרָשָׁע וְאוֹי לִשְׁכֵנוֹ" (*Sukkah* 56b). As a matter of fact, *Chazal* tell us that the reason Reubenites joined Korach's rebellion against Moshe and Aharon (*Bamidbar* 16:1) is that the tribe of Reuben, while wandering in the Sinai desert, resided in close proximity to the Kehatites, of which Korach was a family member. "How wise are the words of our sages!" — "כַּמָּה גְדוֹלִים דִּבְרֵי חֲכָמִים" (*Shabbos* 12b).

Immediately, I wrote a four-page letter to Suzie, expressing my deep disappointment regarding her ill-intended step. I made every attempt to arouse within her the same religious convictions that had permeated her very being while she was with us in Sweden.

I then attempted to appeal to her conscience. I stressed the fact that she lost both of her parents solely because they were Jews. Thus, they died *al kiddush Hashem*, for the sanctification of Hashem's name. "If you now turn away from your religion and that of your parents," I wrote to her, "their death will become meaningless. They will have died for naught."

Although the Nazis lost the war and did not become the dominating power on earth, they, unfortunately, succeeded partially in at least one area. Hitler's ardent desire to make the Jews disappear from the face of the earth was indeed partially realized, as we lost approximately 40 percent of our people to his evil actions. Six million out of a total Jewish world population of 15 million perished at his hands. Each Jew now leaving the fold places an additional feather in the cap of Hitler and his cohorts, as he helps to make the world more *Judenrein*.

Although her children will technically be considered Jews according to Torah law, I further advised Suzie that for all practical purposes, they would be lost to the Jewish people. Reliable statistics clearly indicate that even when the mother of a mixed marriage is of the Jewish faith, the overwhelming majority of their children remain uncommitted and eventually follow Christian dogma or they follow no religion at all. "Are you prepared to abandon even the secular Judaism in which your parents raised you?" I inquired. I concluded my letter with the fervent hope and prayer that she would be able to rescind and abrogate her commitment to the Italian boy, and retain her obligations to her fellow Jews.

Suzie's response arrived almost two weeks later. Her tear-stained letter began, "Dear Serena: I hate you." She then related that when she completed reading my letter she wept uncontrollably and uninterruptedly. The letter had stirred her emotionally and aroused within her a guilty conscience that was so severe that she decided to break off her relationship with the Italian boy. As a result, even her own relatives, who had apparently endorsed the intermarriage, were now so agitated about its cancellation that they completely abandoned Suzie to a life of solitude, to be all alone in the world.

In my next letter to Suzie, I attempted to raise her spirits. "I am confident," I wrote to her, "that Hashem will not forsake you. He has helped you overcome your illness, and he will surely help you again. One must never lose faith in Hashem. In due time, you will find your *chasan* and you will yet enjoy a pleasant and fulfilling life."

Several weeks later, Suzie mailed me a photo of herself with a nice young Jewish man. "This is the boy I plan to marry with the help of Hashem," was her joyous announcement.

Where is Suzie now? I still retain the photo, but by the time I came to the United States in August 1948, I had misplaced her address. Much to my chagrin, I have lost all contact with her.

MEANWHILE, BACK IN RAMLOSA BRUN, I WAS STILL A sick girl, suffering from both pneumonia and tuberculosis. My

What of My Own Family?

older sister Fayge often telephoned from the convalescent home where she was recuperating from the many illnesses she had endured. Once, she informed me that numerous lists had been distributed among the patients, listing the names of some people who had survived the concentration camps. In perusing these lists meticulously, she discovered, on one particular list, the name of an individual whom we knew personally back home in Tornalya. She immediately sent a telegram to him, asking him if he knew whether any of our family members had returned to Tornalya.

Shortly thereafter, Fayge received a telegram from Uncle Menashe, who was my father's youngest brother. In the year 1944, he had been recruited for forced labor. When he was eventually placed on a train headed in the direction of Auschwitz, he managed to jump off the train and spent the remainder of the war hiding in the nearby forests. When he was later asked what he ate in the forests, he would humorously and wittily reply that he ate everything that didn't eat him! After the war, having lost his wife and his two children, he returned to Tornalya and rented a tiny apartment. He also opened a diminutive tailor shop, which enabled him to eke out a meager existence. He realized then and there that his future did not lie in Tornalya. He was determined to immigrate to *Eretz Yisrael* — even by illegal means, if that was the only possibility.

Uncle Menashe's telegram simply informed us, my sister reported, that he was residing in Tornalya and that our two brothers, Zalmen and Chaim Leib, were with him. Choking with emotion and in a trembling voice I asked, "And nothing about our parents and nothing about the rest of the family?" My sister responded that the telegram did not mention anything about them. She tried to infuse me with hope that we would hear from them yet.

I was in a state of utter shock, of profound depression. I dragged myself to my bed, threw myself on it, and began to cry bitterly. I felt as if the bottom had dropped out of my life. This was surely the end, I thought. To continue to live without my parents was unimaginable. All of my hopes, plans, and visions for the future seemed to have suddenly disintegrated into thin air.

My mind, at the time, treated the apparent loss of my father quite differently from the apparent loss of my mother. When I first became aware of the gas chambers and crematoria at Auschwitz, I greeted those reports as highly exaggerated. I felt that they were misleading and a misrepresentation of the true facts. In my wildest imagination, I could not fathom the possibility of human beings behaving like untamed savages and uncivilized barbarians. However, with the passage of time and the many atrocities exposed by the Allied armies as they occupied the concentration camps, the incredible and unbelievable became actual and real. I now fully understood what Mengele's selection process at the Auschwitz gates was all about. The elderly arrivals, the young children, the weaker and sickly ones, those who were considered to be too feeble to join labor groups and to produce for the Third Reich, were scheduled for immediate execution. Thus, gradually, the sick feeling overcame us that perhaps we would never again see our mother, our two younger brothers, and our sister again. We grudgingly acknowledged this apparent fact. Thus, their failure to return to Tornalya was perhaps something we had already silently foreseen and acceded to. It was sad and depressing, but the shock was not too severe.

The situation was quite different in my father's case. He had been selected in Auschwitz for physical labor. He was generally a strong and healthy individual. I was confident that if my sisters and I had survived the camps, he certainly must have survived. I always imagined that he would be the first of the family to return to our home. Perhaps, I thought, the loss of his wife and his three youngest children broke his gentle heart and contributed to his demise. However, his failure to return home was so unexpected that it augmented my emotional depression and my feeling of melancholy.

Our father left us many legacies. He was known as an outstanding *talmid chacham* and a giant in *yiras shamayim* (fear of Hashem). Utterly modest and humble, he came to be loved and admired by people in every walk of life. Observant and non-religious Jews alike were proud and happy to count him as a friend. He always strove to help not only his own family members, but also other Jews in any way possible. He would listen attentively as someone poured out his troubles and heartaches, and would share his friend's burdens to the point that his own distress was readily apparent. Another person's joy was his joy.

Our father's wisdom knew no bounds. At all times we trusted his judgment, as he always seemed to know the proper path for us to follow. For us, his word was final and we happily abided by it. He can truly be referred to as a *tzaddik*, a genuinely righteous man of piety in every fiber of his being, with hardly a trace of materialistic concern — indeed, with no thought but concern for his family and friends.

Our mother was the most unselfish and generous woman I ever knew. Her sole concern in this world was the welfare of her husband and children and to them she dedicated all of her efforts. Three of her 11 pregnancies had ended in miscarriages. Yet, despite her physical weakness and occasional ailments, I rarely saw her sitting idle. The very idea of relaxing was foreign to her. She did everything with so much intensity.

Since she was in charge of managing the family's financial dealings, virtually all of our savings were put aside to secure dowries for the four girls of the family. In Eastern Europe in those days, it was difficult to arrange for a daughter's marriage without contributing an adequate and sufficient dowry.

Our mother shared all of our father's *hashkafos* on Judaism and helped implement them to the fullest extent. She was constantly on the alert, especially when our father was not present, and in a pleasant and cheerful manner made sure that we were conducting ourselves in the ways of Torah and *mitzvos*. She was a highly conscientious woman and proved to be the perfect companion for a man of my father's caliber.

Three other members of our immediate family perished at the hands of the Nazis. After a brief stay in Auschwitz, their lights were extinguished. They became part of the six million Jewish victims.

My brother Avraham was a kind, goodhearted, and most unselfish youngster. From brief conversations with him people were able to note his sharp intellect. My father was proudly able to prognosticate his future as a true *talmid chacham*. He certainly had the potential. When we were incarcerated in the Tornalya ghetto and were forced to ration our meager bread supplies, Avraham would generally not consume his own portion, but rather would put it aside. Then, whenever the younger children cried from hunger, he would graciously offer them his bread and persuade them to accept it.

My sister Mindel was a pretty and loving young girl who was very close to my heart. She was an extremely bright girl. When she was only two years old, I began to spend much of my time with her. How she loved those bedtime stories I used to tell! Since my mother became pregnant and was sick at the time, I took on myself the responsibility to brush Mindel's beautiful blonde hair, dress her, and assist her with everything she needed. As a result, her love for me was immeasurable. She felt so close to me, almost as if I was her mother.

Moshe Shmuel was the youngest of our family. He was merely a child of five when we were torn apart. He possessed such a warm personality. He was precious and we all loved him so. It still boggles my mind when I attempt to comprehend why such an innocent youngster, one who had never hurt anyone, should be incarcerated and eventually murdered. Only a sub-human creature, a fiendish savage, could ever perpetrate a crime of this magnitude.

While I was still weeping and mourning the loss of so many loved ones, my roommate, Kitty W., came over and inquired about my problem. Why was I crying so uncontrollably? When I informed her that we had just received the news that only two of my brothers had returned home, whereas my parents and the rest of the family had apparently perished at the hands of the Nazis, she screamed at me angrily, "Aren't you ashamed of yourself? Show me one other person who has five family members who survived!"

Although the problems of others did not really alleviate my own pain and sorrow, I nevertheless ceased crying in the open. I felt that I had no right to do anything to anger others who were experiencing the same or even worse, plight and predicament as we were (according to the *Midrash, Devarim* 2:22); however, a pain shared by many does, in fact, lighten the pain (see also *Chinuch, Mitzvah* 331).

My nerves were so shattered by recent events that on the following Yom Kippur, I actually prayed to Hashem to take my life, as I was unable to cope with the tremendous mental anguish I had to endure. I then remembered my father's teachings that everyone is born for a specific purpose, and that wishing and praying for death is considered a violation of Torah. I experienced a sudden feeling of remorse and penitence, and prayed to Hashem that he remove this excruciating pain and mental agony from my heart.

A NEW ACQUAINTANCE NOW SHIFTED THE FOCUS OF my thoughts in a different direction, one that somehow would

New Family tend to lighten and alleviate the mental anguish I was suffering. My feelings of charity and mercy were vigorously marshaled as I noticed a young girl in such misery that she required immediate sympathy and compassion from another human being.

There was an empty bed near mine. A nurse entered the room; in her arms, she carried a little girl, whom she placed on the empty bed. The girl cried so hard and with such hopeless-sounding sobs that I was heartbroken. I wanted to help her in every way possible, but I did not know what to do.

I sat down on her bed, leaned over, and began to talk. I began to tell her about my family, about my parents, my brothers and sisters. I talked about my grandparents and my cousins. I never mentioned the fact that many of them had been annihilated by Hitler's hordes. I told her how wonderful and admirable these people were, and about the places where they resided. I noticed that the girl had stopped crying and was listening to me intently.

Suddenly, she interrupted me. "Excuse me," she said, "did you say you had an uncle in Vishny Verecky?"

When I responded in the affirmative, she informed me that Vishny Verecky was her hometown, and she distinctly remembered that a certain Yisroel Hershkowitz often visited their home.

"Is it possible that we are related?" she excitedly asked, with a feeling expressing both hope and anticipation. "Perhaps Hashem has sent you to me to let me know that I am not alone in this world, bereft of any family members. I now have you!"

She then told me all about her parents and her four little brothers. I related to her that several years ago, I, too, had visited Vishny Verecky, and I could vividly recall being in their home and seeing young children playing on the floor.

Surie Weiss

However, I could not state, with any amount of certainty, that we were actually related. I suggested that I write to my aunt in the United States, as she would be more proficient in shedding light on this matter. I immediately fired off a letter to my aunt.

Both of us waited anxiously and impatiently for her reply, which reached us within a week. This letter included the usual $10, plus an additional $5 for my newly discovered friend, whose name was Surie Weiss. We were indeed closely related, my aunt wrote. She explained that Surie's mother was her cousin. Since Surie's mother was already orphaned at the time of her marriage, my aunt informed us, she herself had escorted her to the *chupah*, serving as her *unterfuehrer*.

One cannot possibly describe the joy and the delight we experienced on that day. It was as if we had been showered with a special gift from Heaven. We were emotionally overcome. We hugged and kissed incessantly. And why not? Now we were not only devoted friends, but we were also actually related! In spite of our despondent plight, the entire world appeared to have become a better place for us. From then on, we became inseparable. Together, our dreams, hopes, and visions for the future appeared greatly enhanced.

Although I was several years older than Surie, I looked

much younger than my age, so many people actually thought we were twins. During our long ordeal with tuberculosis, both of us had become extremely slender and our heights were approximately the same. However, since I had already reached my full potential height before our confinement, whereas Surie's height had not yet reached its full potential (her growth being temporarily stunted by the Nazi persecutions and tortures) she continued to grow, and eventually became several inches taller than me.

My friendship with Surie continued to grow and develop by leaps and bounds. I could not have loved her more even if we had been sisters. I often expressed to her my fervent hope that perhaps someday she would marry one of my older brothers, and then she would become part of our immediate family. It was merely a dream at the time, a visionary creation of my wishful imagination.

Who could have imagined at the time that this dream would eventually become an actual reality? It was so far-fetched, so artificial, and so illusory. Yet within a few short years, the unimaginable occurred, as Surie married my brother Chaim Leib!

Since my health continued to improve rapidly and I had completely recovered from the pneumonia that had plagued me for so long, my cousin and I, who had also made excellent progress, were transferred to a place called Ribingelund. Here, my younger sister Golde joined us. The facilities at Ribingelund had originally been constructed to serve as army barracks, and they had been converted to a hospital. The beds were hospital beds, and 30 girls shared a room. Many girls had arrived in Ribingelund suffering from tuberculosis. Many doctors and nurses frequented the facilities, which certainly augmented our trust and confidence. We all felt that here they would be able to tend to our needs on a more individual basis, and the results did not disappoint us. We were all so grateful to the Swedish

Jewish patients at the clinic in Arkiva, Sweden.
In bottom row left – a picture of myself and my sister Golde

government who had so generously provided us with these facilities.

Since all of the girls had, at least, partially recuperated prior to their arrival at Ribingelund, it was no longer necessary to serve us meals in our beds. Instead, we ate at tables in the hospital dining room. Across the table from me, I noticed a young and extremely pretty girl. Her name was Esther J. She, too, had once suffered from a touch of tuberculosis, but fortunately, she had made a complete recovery. She was still in the hospital for the sole purpose of observation, to assure that her recuperation was indeed total.

When I discovered that Esther was dating a Swedish-born German boy, I began talking to her during the next meal. I first inquired as to her hometown. Where did she come from? I discovered that I knew her grandparents quite well as they lived in a town close to my hometown. In fact, I had spent several weeks at their home. Her grandfather had been a well-known Rav. She stared at me with a feeling of both disbelief and insolence when she heard this, and then hurriedly left the table.

At the following meal, she seated herself at another table, and with a voice filled with rage and indignation, she screamed at me, "If you are so religious why are you eating *treifah* food? You're not really religious, are you?" she railed.

I attempted to explain to her that the Torah was given to live with (*Yoma* 85b). One may violate all laws of the Torah (except the three cardinal sins) in order to preserve one's life. If I could not eat, I would surely die. When I got well with the help of Hashem,

Head doctor Von-Rosen in Ribingelund, Sweden

I had every intention of consuming only kosher food, I assured her. Again, she hastened from the table. I noticed that she was weeping uncontrollably, shedding bitter tears.

I never ever mentioned to her that I was aware that she was dating a German boy. Also, I certainly never reprimanded her for this action; therefore, I could not quite comprehend why Esther felt so estranged and alienated from me, an estrangement that often bordered on outright anger and fury. What exactly annoyed her about me? How had I harmed her?

At the next meal, she sat at my table once again, and I resolved to confront her with my dilemma as to why she appeared so angry with me. In a sullen and morose voice, she confided in me that she had been dating a German gentile for some time and she planned to marry him. "I am the only survivor of my family and I will not allow my own child to become victims of a mass slaughter the way my family had become," she declared.

"That may truly be your honest opinion," I suggested, "but the possibility also exists that your own children, living as gentiles in a gentile world, would end up killing Jews the same way your boyfriend's parents and grandparents just did in the recent past." At this remark, she instantly burst into tears and abruptly left the dining room area.

I did not see her for several days and was extremely concerned about her apparent mental anguish. Where was she? I wondered. A short time later, she unexpectedly approached me and in an almost inaudible voice, informed me that she had broken up with her boyfriend. She explained that originally she was quite angry with me because when I told her how well I knew her family, it aroused a feeling of guilt within her. At first, she was convinced that marrying a gentile was a step in the right direction. She truly felt that this was the only means of saving her future generations from mass slaughter. However, after hearing me describe her distinguished family in such glowing terms, as a family wholeheartedly committed and dedicated to *Yiddishkeit*, her decision now appeared so wrong and so immoral. She concluded that she was certainly no longer angry with me. On the contrary, she was sincerely grateful to me for having saved her from heading into another tragedy. She was now completely at peace with herself. Several weeks later, she was discharged from the hospital, and I lost contact with her.

Of course, Esther's original plan of intermarriage would not have been the panacea, the cure-all, that she sought, to attain safety and security from the anti-Semites. My husband vividly recalls an incident that occurred in his hometown of Leipzig, Germany. A Jewish tailor once averred confidently that he was not worried about Nazi persecutions. He was married to a Christian woman, and because of her, no Nazi would harm him. My late father-in-law strongly challenged his cocksure position.

The tailor was told in no uncertain terms, that if any harm should befall the Jewish community, he would not be spared. Hiding behind his Christian wife would not guarantee his safety and security. In Hitler's eyes he was a Jew, no matter how far he distanced himself from the Jewish community. One's own Jewishness was all that mattered to him.

My father-in-law's message turned out to be prophetic indeed. Late in 1938, possibly in October or November, Gestapo agents, for reasons unbeknownst to my husband, arrested the tailor. When his family left Germany in April 1939, the tailor's whereabouts were still unknown. At the time of his arrest, mass deportations to concentration camps had not yet begun. The tailor's arrest and deportation were among the earliest recorded in Leipzig.

After having stayed in Ribingelund for approximately nine months, we were moved to the northern region in Sweden, to a town called Haellnaes in the province of Vaesterbotten, less than 10 miles from the border of Lapland. It lies in the extreme northern part of Europe, above the Arctic Circle. The region that makes up Lapland belongs to Norway, Sweden, Finland, and Russia. We found many Lapps residing in Haellnaes.

Lapland has an extremely cold climate. Winter lasts nine months of the year. The other three months resemble spring in areas that have mild climates. Because Lapland lies so far north, it has a period of two months in the summer when the sky never darkens. On the other hand, the sun never rises above the horizon for two months each winter.

We arrived in Haellnaes in the middle of the winter. There was snow everywhere, in some places as much as six feet high. The children dug tunnels in the snow and under the top level as well. During the two hours of daylight, we went for long walks. We were dressed warmly, the air was dry, and there was practically no wind, so we did not feel cold at all. Only our eyelashes became white and long, due to the icicles formed by the freezing of the vapors from our breath. We saw some Lapps on sleds being pulled by dogs, swishing by. They traveled at such speeds that it actually appeared as if they were flying.

At Haellnaes, we were also provided with some amateur entertainment presented by the nurses. During one particular performance, an adult Lapp woman performed as a child. It was most amusing and enjoyable for us. At least for a short period of time, these performances helped divert us from our personal problems.

After the winter months passed, the days became longer. In the month of May, we already experienced long days and short nights. The snow melted in those places where most of it had been shoveled away, and beautiful flowers were blooming next to the snow. The entire area was saturated with a glowing and blazing splendor. It was a glorious scene, delightful to the eye. In the month of July, the weather was comfortably warm, but never really intensively hot, and the daylight lasted 22 hours.

On one particular afternoon, a gentleman arrived in Haellnaes and presented himself as the Stockholm synagogue's chief cantor. The purpose of his trip to the distant Lapland area was to entertain the patients at the hospital with a concert of Jewish songs and liturgical music. He possessed a sweet and powerful voice, and we all enjoyed his performance. When one of the girls requested that he sing the Christian religious song "Ave Maria," however, he refused. He explained that he was a cantor, a Jewish religious official, and it did not behoove him to sing anything which runs contrary to the Jewish religion.

A completely different story was reported of this cantor as he visited Varnama, a Swedish camp populated mostly by religious refugees from Czechoslovakia. "Girls," he said, "I hear that a number of you refuse to eat the meat served here because it is not kosher. Forget all that nonsense. The Judaism you remember is gone forever. It's old fashioned and obsolete and it does not exist any more. You may eat any kind of meat you like without the slightest hesitation." When some of the girls questioned him as to how *treifah* meat could be "kosher," when everyone knows that Jews have special laws about kosher slaughter, he replied that there were simply no longer any *shochtim*, as they had all been killed by the Nazis. "But it's really no problem," he said, "as there is no shortage of meat in Sweden."

The girls were terribly confused. They had always learned that for centuries, Jews had made countless sacrifices to keep the Torah's commandments. As for the cantor, who now represented himself as a rabbi, he looked very different from those they remembered from home. But wasn't everything different now? Maybe this rabbi was right. Had they not seen with their own eyes how the Nazis annihilated untold numbers of pious Jews? Perhaps all of the *shochtim* were, indeed, really gone!

The so-called rabbi then concluded, "You, my dear girls, are young, you have your whole lives ahead of you. Join us and we will help you, you can all build new lives, married to fine young Swedish men. Forget the past, and you need never again be persecuted as Jews."

Compounding the confusion of the girls was the fact that, as part of his performance, the so-called rabbi (who was actually a Reform cantor) chanted *Kol Nidrei*. The melody was beautiful and the rendition impressive. But why *Kol Nidrei* then?

Among the girls were two sisters named Brachie and Bayle. They found themselves unable to believe the words of the so-called rabbi. They remembered the Rav in their prewar community, a pious and scholarly Jew, the antithesis of this person who was encouraging them to eat *treifah* meat and marry non-Jews. They decided to write to their uncle, Rav Dushinsky in *Eretz Yisrael*, and ask for his opinion.

Rav Dushinsky, who was the leader of Jerusalem's *Eidah Hachareidis*, immediately assessed the situation and contacted Rav Benjamin Ze'ev Jacobson, who was a prominent personality in Orthodox European Jewry. In the past, he had been the Rav of the Machzikei Hadas community in Copenhagen,

R' Yosef Zvi Dushinsky

Denmark, and at the time, he resided in Sweden. Rav Jacobson got in touch with the girls at once and invited them to Lidingo, where an Orthodox school for girls had been founded by the renowned and highly dedicated Torah pioneer, Horav Shlomo Wolbe. Several other girls who hesitated to accept the arguments of the cantor joined them.

Unfortunately, however, Brachie, Bayle, and their friends were exceptions. Most of the other girls, traumatized by the suffering they had endured and vulnerable without their lost families, were taken in, and unwittingly resigned themselves to a life far removed from traditional Judaism. It should be noted that the cantor, of course, had come to the camps on behalf of the Reform community's rabbi, Dr. Ehrenpreis, who exerted every effort to estrange and to alienate Jews from their traditions.

As a matter of fact, when Dr. Ehrenpreis first learned of plans to open a strictly Orthodox school for girls near Stockholm, this Reform rabbi did everything in his power to sabotage the project, calling on all of his own and his congregation's long-standing government connections to participate in his endeavor to stunt the growth of true *Yiddishkeit* in Sweden. Reinforcing the refugees' Jewish identity through institutions like the proposed school could lead to a new wave of anti-Semitism, they argued. Instead, the government should encourage the girls' speedy assimilation into the local non-Jewish community.

Immediate steps were taken to counteract the damaging activities of Dr. Ehrenpreis. Rav Pinchos Wohlgelernter, emissary of the American *Agudas Harabbanim* to the Stockholm *Vaad Hahatzalah*, stepped into the fray. He made the rounds of the government officials, persuading them to keep their original promises to the *Vaad*. Despite the vicious slanders heaped on him by Dr. Ehrenpreis and his congregation, he persisted in his efforts until the new school in Lidingo, with the full sanction of the Swedish government, was an accomplished fact.

Near the end of the summer, we were again transferred to southern Sweden, to a city called Arvika. The doctors at Arvika became slightly impatient and somewhat irritated by the slow progress I was making on the road to recovery. I actually did not feel sick at all and for all practical purposes, was ready to be discharged. But since my condition continued to be infectious, I was not permitted to leave the sanitarium grounds.

One day, the doctor summoned me to his office and recommended that I undergo surgery. The doctors would collapse a part of the infected section of my lung so that the lung would not be functioning temporarily, and thus, would be able to heal properly. My initial gut reaction was to refuse even to consider the process. I had seen others who had undergone this operation whose bodies now stooped, often bending at the knees simultaneously, as they attempted to walk. I certainly did not want to find myself in such an inferior physical condition for the rest of my life. Therefore, I remained adamant and inflexible and courteously declined to consent to this surgical process.

Physicians had often advised me that total recovery lay in my own hands. It was all up to me. If I were to eat in sufficient amounts and gain some weight, my condition would improve immeasurably. I now felt that this then was my solemn duty and obligation. I simply had to gain weight. My cousin Surie had given me an added purpose in life. I felt that I was responsible for her welfare and that I had to get well, even if only for her sake.

I decided to eat everything that my physicians recommended. I ate even when I did not feel especially hungry. My older sister wrote to me that she knew a gentleman who resided in Landskrona who had suffered from tuberculosis and never had much of an appetite. His rabbi advised him to beat two eggs together with a whole lemon, add two tablespoons of sugar, and drink the mixture once daily. The man related to my sister that this mixture really stimulated his appetite to the extent that he voraciously began eating everything placed before him on the table. I too, decided to try the rabbi's remedy. During meals, I meticulously observed the amounts others were consuming and practically forced myself to eat the same amounts. I started to gain weight and my health improved dramatically.

AT THIS POINT, WHAT WAS HAPPENING WITH THE other surviving members of our immediate family? My older

More Family News

sister, who had been recuperating in a convalescent home, would occasionally come to visit me in the sanitarium at Ramlosa Brun. There she met a young man, a survivor of the infamous Lodz ghetto, who had taken it upon himself to supply the patients with their religious needs. He brought us *siddurim* and *chumashim*. On Rosh Hashanah, he blew the *shofar* for us, and on Sukkos he came to us with the required *arba minim*. His enthusiasm and exuberance in helping others perform *mitzvos* knew no bounds. His name was Shlomo Zalmen Gotheil.

He and my sister developed a relationship, as his ardent interest and zeal to perform *mitzvos* reminded her of her own father, who had been similarly inclined. They were eventually married in Landskrona, and Harav Jacobson performed the wedding. The fact that my doctors permitted me to travel to Landskrona to attend the wedding ceremony was a clear indication to me that my condition was no longer contagious. With the help of Hashem, I was well on my way to total recovery.

My older brother, Zalmen, succeeded with much adroitness and ingenuity in evading the concentration camps, but endured many hardships along the way. At the end of the war, he returned to our home in Coltova, fervently hoping to reunite with other family members. However, much to his dismay, he discovered that both our house and the adjoining *shul* had been utterly destroyed. A Christian neighbor later informed us that a major battle had been fought in that vicinity between German and Russian forces, and that a bomb of unknown origin had exploded on our house. None of the other houses in Coltova appeared to have been damaged during that major battle. How ironic!

Since our parents had owned a house in nearby Tornalya, my brother then traveled there, only to find that the house was now occupied by strangers. The mayor appeared genuinely interested in my brother's plight, however, and promised to have the illegal occupants evicted. My brother was instructed to return on the following day to receive all the legal documents necessary to reoccupy the premises. Meanwhile, though, the mayor ascertained that one of his closest assistants had chosen to reside in the house, so when my brother returned on the following day to receive the documents, he was literally thrown out of the mayor's office without any semblance of an explanation. My brother now realized that even after Germany's total collapse, anti-Semitism was still as rampant as ever in our home community. He became utterly disgusted with Tornalya, and decided to immigrate to *Eretz Yisrael* or Palestine, as it was then known.

The task of immigrating to Palestine was not an easy one. The Palestine-bound masses of Jewish survivors, however, were not deterred by either temporary zones of the victorious armies in Europe, or by mandatory immigration rules. In the light of the conviction of so many Jews that Palestine was as Jewish as England was English, all policies, laws, and administrative regulations lost their deterrent aspect as ethical barriers.

They appeared merely as irritating and unjust obstacles to their hope for a new beginning.

Running the blockade became a deadly serious business. An organization called *Bericha* sprang into being. It was dedicated to achieving a mass exodus of desperate Jews from Europe to Palestine. *Bericha* meant long-distance marches for men, women, and children, across fields, rivers, and mountains, across the boundaries of countries and states, and across territories saturated with contesting armies. For its commanders, *Bericha* meant selecting routes that were not easily detected by police, border guards, informers, and soldiers; routes that were passable even at night. It meant providing shelter, food, medical care, identity papers, trucks, trains, and ships. It meant a considerable amount of contact with civilian and military authorities, unofficial diplomacy, much initiative, and a great deal of resolution and daring.

When the stream of illegal immigration to Palestine assumed mass proportions, the British government forcibly transferred thousands of survivors to deportation ships and sent them to detention camps in Cyprus. The total number arriving in 1946 was approximately 51,000. In the camps, they were assisted by Jewish emissaries in the organization of health and education facilities. They also received some military training.

My brother also participated in the treacherous journey to southern Italy, where a ship would transfer him to Palestine. Unfortunately, however, the British navy intercepted his ship and he was interned in Cyprus. He became seriously ill in the internment camp, and a young survivor named Fayge Weinberger, who was also interned in the camp, nursed him back to health. Eventually, they were married in a Cyprus ceremony. With the establishment of the State of Israel, they were released and quickly absorbed in the mainstream of mass immigration that began to arrive in the country. My brother joined the army and fought valiantly in Israel's war of liberation.

My younger brother, Chaim Leib, spent one week of his confinement together with my father at Auschwitz. From there, he was sent to Buena and then was transferred to the notorious camp at Buchenwald. At war's end, he found himself in Theresienstadt, where he was eventually liberated.

Soon after liberation, my brother decided to head home to Coltova. He boarded a train in the city of Terezin (near Theresienstadt) going to Prague, the capital of Czechoslovakia, a distance of no more than one hour. In Prague, he planned to change trains and head in the direction of Tornalya. At the Prague railroad station, ambulances were waiting for him and for several other former *Haeftlinge*. They were driven to a local hospital for a thorough physical checkup, which lasted for several days. It was determined that my brother was merely suffering from a case of extreme fatigue, and he was told that a long period of rest was essential for his well-being. My brother now felt free to continue his journey to Tornalya.

It should be pointed out at this time that *Haeftlinge* were permitted to travel on Czech and Hungarian trains without any charge whatsoever. Perhaps, seeing the physical condition of these downtrodden and abused *Haeftlinge* created a feeling of guilt among the native population. What had they done to them? How could they provide adequate restitution?

The train left Prague headed for Pressburg, now called Bratislava. Since my brother was extremely hungry by then, he entered a local restaurant, introduced himself as a former *Haeftling* who did not have a penny to his name, and was treated to a lavish meal, without any charge. The restaurateur displayed absolutely no anti-Semitic tendencies during his brief encounter with my brother, and acted with a genuine feeling of friendship and mutual respect. My brother was most grateful for the meal and for the gracious manner in which it was extended to him. Now, off to Tornalya, he decided.

Since there were no trains available to Tornalya, he decided to take a detour and boarded a train headed for Budapest, the capital of Hungary. In Budapest, he boarded yet another train, which took him to the village of Banreve, at the Hungarian-Slovakian border, less than 10 kilometers from his ultimate destination. Since there was not sufficient space inside the train as it was packed to capacity, my brother was forced to travel on top of the train.

The short trip from Budapest to Banreve took almost one day to complete. The train traveled at a snail's pace, making unscheduled stops at every town and village in its path. It was indeed an arduous and suspenseful journey. At times, one could actually walk faster than the moving train. Finally, an exhausted Chaim Leib arrived in Banreve. Rather than search for new means to transport him to Tornalya, he decided to proceed to Tornalya on foot.

How great was his disappointment when he entered Tornalya! The first question he tearfully posed to his brother Zalmen was, "Is *Tatty* here?" When he received a negative reply, he burst into uncontrollable tears. His world, for all practical purposes, seemed to have ended. He had come to Tornalya to be reunited with his immediate family. He felt they could start a new life. Now, he was suddenly confronted with a resounding, no! It was no longer possible. Our world would never be the same again. He was both horrified and dismayed. He was frustrated. What could he do now?

For the time being, he moved into the house that Uncle Menashe had rented. Both he and Zalmen now resided there. Meanwhile, his brain was working overtime contemplating his next move. He realized immediately that Tornalya was now devoid of any Jewish content. Its Jewish inhabitants had been barbarously massacred. Therefore, it certainly was not a place where he could remain for long. His initial consideration was to immigrate to *Eretz Yisrael* together with Zalmen. However, when the gratifying news reached him that three of his sisters had survived and were recuperating in Sweden, his immediate move became crystal clear to him. He would go to Sweden.

Since our *shul* in Coltova had not been destroyed, Chaim Leib and Zalmen searched the *shul*'s attic for the items our parents had secretly hidden there. They were able to uncover my older sister's complete dowry, which included embroidered tablecloths, several bushels of wheat, and many other valuable items. Since my brothers' plight was desperate indeed, and they had no other means to sustain themselves, they sold some of these items to local citizens. Chaim Leib intended to use part of this income to help him reach the shores of Sweden.

At this time, the Bergen-Belsen camp had been converted to a major health center, which catered to the many physical needs of its survivors. Once in Bergen-Belsen, arrangements could be made to reach Sweden with the Swedish government's consent and financial support. Chaim Leib now decided to head to Bergen-Belsen.

In Bergen-Belsen, he underwent a thorough checkup and, unexpectedly, his case was diagnosed as a touch of tuberculosis. Surgery was performed on him to ease a minor problem in this regard. King Gustavus's offer of opening the gates of Sweden to all holocaust victims who sought to recover from serious diseases was now extended to Chaim Leib. A short time thereafter, he landed in Sweden.

When Chaim Leib visited me at the sanitarium in Arvika in December 1946, I could hardly recognize him. The last time I had seen him, in June 1944, he was short, somewhat chubby, with light skin and light brown hair. Now, a tall young man with a dark complexion and black hair had entered my room. To my first words to him, "My, how you have changed!" he humorously responded that suffering had apparently darkened his appearance.

The Swedish government had done everything humanly possible to help us regain our health. The Swedes also took a genuine interest in helping us live productive lives. Realizing that most of us would not remain in Sweden forever and would eventually immigrate to the United States, they began to prepare us for the future by offering us lessons in English. A young Swedish gentleman, who was highly proficient in English, became the tutor, and he performed his duties admirably. Many girls joined his classes, eager to learn the language. Again, I gratefully offer my thanks to King Gustavus V, whose vision made these classes possible. They were certainly instrumental in teaching me the basics of English, thus making my first weeks in the United States more pleasant. This righteous gentile had certainly earned a place in the world to come (*Tosefta, Sanhedrin,* Chapter 13 and *Maimonides, Laws of Repentance,* Chapter 3). Grateful Jewish people will forever remember him.

When our cousin Surie was well enough to be discharged from the sanitarium, we promised each other to keep in touch and never lose contact. She too, went to Landskrona, and moved in with my older sister. When my younger sister was then discharged, I felt rather lonely. I knew, however, that my health had also improved and that my own discharge was not far away. I was finally discharged in the early spring of 1948, and I, too, went to Landskrona.

CHAPTER 8
A NEW LIFE

MY YOUNGER SISTER AND SURIE HAD RENTED a room in an apartment house in Landskrona and I moved into the room with them. A Jewish-Swedish organization, whose name I now cannot remember, paid our rent and all our other living expenses. Since my older sister had given birth to a baby boy, there was absolutely no room for us in her tiny apartment. My brother also had rented a room in our apartment house. Though our sleeping quarters were separate, we nevertheless ate all of our meals together.

Meanwhile, my uncle and aunt from Gary, Indiana, had sent the required affidavit to enable us to enter the United States. My older sister's family was the first to receive their American visas, and they left Sweden in the early summer. The aid organization hired an attorney to handle our immigration situation; he suggested that we come to his office in Goteborg for an extremely urgent meeting.

When we arrived in Goteborg, the attorney informed us that it was imperative that we leave for the United States expeditiously, without any further delay. It had become new U.S. policy to have each potential immigrant X-rayed. Even though we had recovered from our illnesses, tuberculosis leaves a permanent stain on the lungs and we might not pass the U.S. examination. However, if we expedited matters, we could always tell the authorities that we were unaware of this newly adopted X-ray law.

The attorney then dispatched a telegram to Gary informing my uncle and aunt of the situation. Either we would leave immediately or we would not be able to leave at all. Passage must also be booked on the Swedish steamship "Stockholm," because it was scheduled to leave within a week. Since the "Stockholm" was leaving on her maiden voyage, the attorney emphasized, its prices would be exorbitant. My uncle and aunt complied fully with the directives of the attorney, telegraphed the necessary funds, and within a week we were on our way to the United States. We arrived in August 1948.

Leaving Surie behind was a most painful experience. With tearful good-byes, we promised each other that we would do everything possible to get together again. We would leave no stone unturned, aiming to reach this goal.

The "S.S. Stockholm" was a beautiful ship, and all of its facilities were brand new. When we left Sweden in August, the weather was a little on the cool side and we were wearing spring coats. The temperature rose several degrees as we sailed further away from Sweden, but it never became intensely hot. We truly enjoyed our journey under clear blue skies and on a ship equipped with all modern facilities.

When we finally arrived in the United States and completed the long and arduous immigration process, I hailed a taxi and asked the driver to take us to the railroad station. We were heading for Gary, Indiana. I felt somehow quite shaky with my limited knowledge of the English language and I was thrilled when I realized that the driver actually understood my directive.

However, quite a different story emerged when we arrived at the railroad station, and I realized that I still had a lot of English to learn. When I asked the driver how much we owed him, he replied, "A dollar and a quarter." I was totally embarrassed. I had absolutely no idea how much to pay. The driver, who was aware of my predicament, removed a dollar and a quarter from his pocket and showed it to me. "Ah! One dollar and 25¢," I said with a sigh of relief. My limited vocabulary had not yet included the word "quarter." Many similar incidents occurred during the next several months, as I spent much of my time attempting to improve my English.

When I finally arrived in Gary, my uncle and aunt treated me as if I was their own child. My aunt took me on a shopping spree and purchased a completely new wardrobe for me. She dressed me from head to toe. My aunt considered the clothes I had brought from Sweden to be old fashioned and inappropriate for me.

I remained in Gary for six weeks; then, I moved to Detroit to live with my older sister. I realized that Gary did not have a strictly Orthodox community. Even members of the Orthodox *shul* did not always comply with basic *halachic* laws and regulations. Many treated *halachah* as a mere menu, from which they would sporadically select items to suit their whim and fancy.

Above all, the time had come for me to find a *chasan*. I had always wanted to marry a *ben Torah*, a yeshiva student. Together, I felt, we would be able, with the help of Hashem, to build a true Jewish home. No such individual existed in Gary. For weeks, my sister in Detroit had been urging me to come to Detroit, since many *b'nai Torah* resided there, and I would surely be able to find an appropriate *shiduch*. I accepted my sister's advice and I came to Detroit right after Yom Kippur.

I was not disappointed. In Detroit I met my husband, and we were married on June 7, 1949. We have been blessed with children, grandchildren, and even great-grandchildren. All of them are living a life of Torah. It has generally been a good life since then.

Occasionally, I continued to have nightmares, frightening dreams accompanied by a sense of oppression, but they decreased as time went on and eventually ceased completely. I still find it difficult to read literature about the gas chambers and crematoria. When we visited the Holocaust Museum in Washington, D.C., I became so restless as I viewed the horrible scenes that I actually trembled and wept. My husband noticed my predicament and strongly urged that we both leave the museum grounds. For a similar reason, we have not yet visited the Museum of Jewish Heritage in New York's Battery Park.

Surie Weiss left Sweden with a children's group and lived in England for one year. She then approached the Joint Distribution Committee and explained to the officers that in England she was all alone, and that she longed to immigrate to the United States, where her only relatives resided. The JDC then graciously arranged for her visa and even paid for all expenses.

We were in New York to attend my younger sister's wedding on the Sunday that Surie arrived. Since I was preoccupied preparing my sister for her wedding, my husband went to the harbor in the late afternoon to pick her up. I was in seventh heaven seeing her again. My husband then commented that he had never ever witnessed such a joyous reunion. Eventually, Surie married my brother Chaim Leib, and we became closely related for life.

MY EXPERIENCES TAUGHT ME SEVERAL LESSONS.
While it may come as a surprise to some, it is a fact that Hitler

The Importance of a Haven was ready and willing to permit the Jews to leave their homes in Germany and in all of the other occupied countries (of course, without their possessions or money). The problem was, however, that no country was willing to accept them. The entrance gates had been tightly locked. Immigration laws and quotas had brought Jewish immigration to other countries to a mere trickle.

In 1917, England had issued the Balfour Declaration, which clearly stated that "His Majesty's Government views with favor the establishment in Palestine of a national home for the Jewish people, and will use their best endeavors to facilitate the achievement of this object." Nevertheless, in May 1939, the British issued the infamous "White Paper," which stated that "His Majesty's Government now declares unequivocally that it is not part of their policy that Palestine should become a Jewish State." As far as further immigration was concerned, the White Paper emphatically declared that "during the next five years, Jewish immigration would be limited to 75,000, bringing the Jewish population up to approximately one third of the total population of Palestine. After the end of the five-year period, no further Jewish immigration would be permitted unless the Arabs of Palestine are prepared to acquiesce to it." Imagine, just 75,000 could come in over a five-year period, while millions stood waiting in the slaughterhouses of Germany and other occupied countries!

Now compare this record to the policy of the established State of Israel. Come one, come all! That policy was declared and became official at the very declaration of statehood. Israel's gates were opened wide. Every Jew was able to return to the land of his ancestors and become a permanent citizen at a moment's notice. Just imagine how many Jews would have survived if an established Jewish state had been in existence! Thus, a Jewish state has become a haven for Jews the world over, and we must do everything possible to assure its safety and security.

AN ADDITIONAL MESSAGE ONE CAN LEARN FROM THE Holocaust is not to rely on the rosy promises of elected officials.

Learning From the Past Often politicians promise us the sky; we trust them, we vote for them, and in the end we are left holding the bag.

Paul Hindenburg was Germany's military leader in World War I. In 1925 he became the first president of the German Republic to be elected by popular vote.

Early in this century, in my husband's hometown, Leipzig, Germany, Chassidic Jews had founded a new *shul* and agreed to name it the Hindenburg Synagogue, in honor of the man who had vanquished a treacherous enemy of the Jews, the Russian Czar. How could anyone at that time have predicted, at the zenith of his political career, when he had been elected German Reichspresident, that he would hand over the reins of the republic and its democratic systems to an ardent racist and vicious anti-Semite?

Hindenburg took command of all German forces in 1916. When the retreating German army approached its own borders, revolutionaries overthrew the Kaiser and sued for peace. Bewildered Germans, fed until then by wartime propaganda telling them of victory and knowing full well that the enemy had not reached their borders when the armistice agreement was signed, wondered who had betrayed them. Their hero was called before a Reichstag committee, but he had a ready answer: "The victorious German army was stabbed in the back by Jews and Socialists." This word, *Dolchstoss* — "dagger blow" — would take its place in the vocabulary of anti-Semitism.

How disappointed were the Jews of the Hindenburg Synagogue! That name of the *shul* was soon forgotten and

Jüdische Mitbürger

Wählt Hindenburg

Wenn Hitler gewählt wird, kommen Faschismus
und Antisemitismus zur Herrschaft

Keiner darf am 10. April an der Wahlurne fehlen

Spenden werden erbeten an die Geschäftsstelle des Hindenburg-Ausschußes Hotel Sachsenhof
(Tel. 20900) oder auf das Postscheck-Konto Leipzig Nr. 52304 (Direktor Otto Weber)

An election poster in the German-Jewish press
urging Jews to vote for Hindenburg rather than for Hitler

rarely ever mentioned. The *shul* was from then on referred to as simply the *vierundzwanzig*, which was the number of its location on the Humboldt Strasse. Only occasionally, from time to time and then only in jest, was the name Hindenburg *shul* ever mentioned again.

Despite the cowardly *Dolchstoss* accusation, in which Hindenburg displayed his total lack of concern for the safety and the welfare of the Jewish population, Jewish citizens were urged by their leaders to cast their vote for Hindenburg when he ran in an election against Hitler. A victorious Hitler, they feared, would increase fascism and anti-Semitism and raise it to catastrophic proportions. Therefore, it was felt that Jews should live up to their civic responsibilities by registering a vote for the lesser of two evils.

There is absolutely no safety and security for Jews in the *galus*. Who could have predicted that Hindenburg's Weimar Republic, a democracy, would someday become Hitler's Third Reich? Can any political leader, even one who pretends to be our friend, really be trusted and counted on? Are they the instruments of our salvation? Most certainly not!

Another case that is proof that we cannot place our faith in politicians or national leaders follows:

As a result of his close connection with the British policy concerning a national Jewish home, Herbert Samuel was appointed the first High Commissioner of Palestine in 1920, thus becoming the first Jew to rule the land in 2,000 years. Samuel was proud of being a Jew. On one particular Shabbos, he walked on foot from his official residence in Jerusalem to the Churva Synagogue to participate in the services. Of course, all honors were accorded to him. He was called to the Torah for the final *aliyah*, the *Maftir*. He recited the *haftarah* and its blessings. When he reached the words that no stranger should ever sit on the throne of King David, "עַל כִּסְאוֹ לֹא יֵשֵׁב זָר," the eyes of many congregants were filled with tears. Here was a man who would surely implement the British Palestine policy. Our 2,000-year-old dream of returning to Zion and Jerusalem was in the process of finally being realized.

But he, too, let us down. In 1922, he excluded the area of Transjordan from the area destined to become the Jewish national home, an exclusion that has implications even today. His efforts to appease Arabs by appointing the young extremist Hajj Amin al Husseini as Mufti of Jerusalem, thus investing him as the highest-ranking Muslim, as well as stopping, and later restricting, Jewish immigration because of Arab pressure, were severely criticized by many Jews. The sharpest critic of Samuel's policy was Vladimir Jabotinsky, but also in the Zionist labor movement, Samuel's policy eventually caused deep disappointment.

One can go on and on, listing the many of our so-called reliable friends, who conveniently absented themselves at crucial times and opted out of their commitments. The list is endless. Experience has taught us that we are virtually alone in this world. As Bil'am so appropriately put it, "...it is a nation that will dwell in solitude ..." — "הֶן עָם לְבָדָד יִשְׁכֹּן" (*Numbers* 23:9).

The Talmud taught us long ago that our only salvation is in the hands of our Father in Heaven (*Sotah* 49a). Therefore, it becomes incumbent on us to fervently pray to Him, to plead with Him and to pour our hearts to Him.

At the same time, one must always remember not to lose hope even in the worst of times. In the most critical and desperate situation, Hashem's mercy may yet shine.

Even if a sharp sword rests on a man's neck, he should not desist from prayer — "אֲפִילוּ חֶרֶב חַדָּה מוּנַחַת עַל צַוָּארוֹ שֶׁל אָדָם אַל יִמְנַע עַצְמוֹ מִן הָרַחֲמִים" (Berachos 10a). Nothing is ever hopeless. Our sages taught us long ago that "the help of Hashem can be immediate: It can come as quickly as the wink of an eye" — "יְשׁוּעַת ה' כְּהֶרֶף עַיִן." This is a key concept of our religion.

The Talmud teaches: "Repentance is so great that it hastens our redemption, as it is written, 'A redeemer shall come forth from Zion to those who repent from willful sin'" — "וּבָא לְצִיּוֹן גּוֹאֵל וּלְשָׁבֵי פֶשַׁע בְּיַעֲקֹב" (Yoma 86b). Let us hope and pray that because of the merits of repentance, Hashem will have mercy on his people, that He will remove us from distress to relief, from darkness to light, and from subjugation to redemption with the coming of the Mashiach.

Chapter 9
DID ANYONE REALLY CARE?

n April 1939, right after the dismemberment of Czechoslovakia, *Fortune* magazine conducted a public opinion poll asking whether a member of Congress should vote yes or no on a bill to open the doors of the United States to refugees from Europe beyond the limits of the immigration quota system. Eighty-three percent voted no, 8.3 percent were undecided, and 8.7 percent voted yes. *Fortune* then commented sadly that an American tradition had been put to rest, repudiated by a large majority. Not only was the quota system never relaxed during the entire period of mass slaughter, but every possible administrative hurdle was placed before the would-be immigrant, so that only a small percentage of the allotted quota was ever used.

This incident, among many others, proved to the Germans that the world was not prepared to help the Jews. On the contrary, such incidents served as actual encouragement to Hitler to go ahead with his plans of extermination.

If any doubts still remained in Hitler's mind as to how other nations would react to his plans, the shameful forms of acquiescence of the American and British governments in the *St. Louis* and *Struma* episodes erased all such doubts.

There is little doubt that the refusal of the Americans to provide even temporary sanctuary to the *St. Louis* refugees amounted to no less than death sentences. As the *St. Louis* was approaching Germany on its return trip, Belgium, Holland, France, and Britain finally took pity on the doomed refugees and jointly found shelter for them in their respective territories. How many of them eventually perished when the German army swept into Western Europe, no one knows. It is a fact, however, that many passengers ultimately perished.

When the U.S. Secretary of State was confronted with the question of why he refused to grant asylum to people whose forced return to Germany meant certain death, he replied with deep patriotic conviction, "I took an oath to protect the flag and obey the laws of my country, and you are asking me to break those laws?" Is there any difference between this argument and that of the Nazi war criminals at the Nuremberg trials who pleaded their innocence because they were committed to their oath to Hitler and their country?

The *Struma*, packed far beyond its capacity with 769 Romanian Jews, sank in the Bosporus on February 24, 1943. Its fate was another indication of the inaction of the civilized world. The *Struma*, which sailed from Romania toward Palestine, was at sea for 74 days, but no country was willing to admit the helpless victims of Nazi persecution. The agonized pleas of its refugees reached the ears of all civilized people during that time, but not their hearts. The British refused to allow them entrance to Palestine, and Turkey did not permit them to disembark. Its 769 men, women, and children perished in the depths of the sea, just a few miles from Istanbul, Turkey.

R' Michael Ber Weissmandel

When it was suggested that the atrocities and persecution perpetrated by the Nazis ought to enlist U.S. humanitarian interest, since we could not be party to any ultimate arrangement that sanctions this kind of cruelty on an organized scale, one high ranking U.S. government official responded that these persecutions were purely a domestic matter, completely within the jurisdiction of Germany. The question remains: Did anyone really care about the Jews?

In 1942, both the U.S. Congress and the British House of Commons finally adopted resolutions condemning Nazi atrocities, but no word was heard about measures to rescue at least part of the doomed people.

In the fall of 1944, the renowned Gaon Harav Michael Ber Weissmandel, an unforgettable hero during the Holocaust period, was placed together with his family and hundreds of other Jews in a temporary camp prior to deportation to Auschwitz. Harav Weissmandel escaped and succeeded in making his way to the residence of the papal nuncio. He described to him the conditions of the families in the camp and asked for his immediate intervention with Jozef Tiso, a Catholic priest who was then the president of Nazi-protected independent Slovakia. Upon Harav Weissmandel's urging, he received the following answer: "This, being Sunday, is a holy day for us. Neither I nor Father Tiso occupy ourselves with profane matters on this day."

When Harav Weissmandel wondered how the blood of children could be considered a profane matter, he was taught a significant chapter in Christian theology. "There is no innocent blood of Jewish children," Rav Weissmandel was told. "All Jewish blood is guilty. You have to die. That is the punishment that has been awaiting you because of the sin you committed in the death of our holy Father." The papal nuncio was, on his holy day, repeating with deep religious conviction

R' Menachem Ziemba

the Hitlerite belief that all Jews are guilty. Hitler believed it on racial grounds, and the papal nuncio did so for theological reasons.

RABBI SHIMON BAR YOCHAI TAUGHT, "IT IS A KNOWN *halachah* that Esau hates Jacob" (*Sifri, Bamidbar,* Chapter 24).

A Halachic View Many commentators have questioned the term *halachah* as used in this context. *Halachah* is a generic term for the entire legal system of Judaism, embracing all the detailed laws and observances. *Halachah* mandates guidelines to the Jews. It teaches a system of conduct to adhere to. The fact that Esau hates Jacob is, therefore, not in the realm of *halachah* per se, but it is rather of a sociological nature, one dealing with social relationships and patterns of collective behavior. The term *halachah*, therefore, appears to be a misnomer in this instance.

The great Gaon Harav Menachem Ziemba, who lost his life in the Warsaw Ghetto uprising, offered a solution to our problem. Let me now attempt to elaborate on it (see *Chiddushei HaGarmaz* Chapter 48). Rabbi Chanina ben Dosa says: "Anyone whose good deeds exceed his wisdom, his wisdom will endure; but anyone whose wisdom exceeds his good deeds, his wisdom shall not endure" — ",כֹּל שֶׁמַּעֲשָׂיו מְרֻבִּין מֵחָכְמָתוֹ חָכְמָתוֹ מִתְקַיֶּמֶת; וְכֹל שֶׁחָכְמָתוֹ מְרֻבָּה מִמַּעֲשָׂיו, אֵין חָכְמָתוֹ מִתְקַיֶּמֶת" (*Pirkei Avos* 3:12). The question is often raised that since a person can act only within the scope of his knowledge and intelligence, how can one's deeds ever exceed one's wisdom?

The Torah informs us that when Hashem offered the Torah to the Jewish people, they unanimously replied: "All that Hashem has said, we shall do and understand." By placing action prior to comprehension, the Israelites removed their right to selection and discretion. Their faith in Hashem was so abundant that they consented to follow His directives blindly, irrespective of their significance and meaning. This unqualified preparedness to do even that which they did not comprehend was tantamount to performing beyond their knowledge. Hence, their deeds, in the form of their readiness, exceeded their wisdom.

Rabban Gamliel, the son of Rabbi Yehudah Hanasi, suggested that this, then, be the blueprint and guideline for all adherents of the Jewish faith. His instructions are as explicit as they are unqualified: "Nullify your will before His will" — "בַּטֵּל רְצוֹנְךָ מִפְּנֵי רְצוֹנוֹ" (*Pirkei Avos* 2:4).

When one discovers that his own will clashes with the views and directives of the Torah, he ought to nullify his will and submit to the will of the Torah. Whether or not one can rationally perceive the wisdom of what he is commanded to do, and even when his will clearly and insistently urges him to head in another direction, Rabban Gamliel still urged that we subject ourselves to the higher authority in Heaven. Ultimately, the test of true faith is its ability to go beyond the rational, the reasonable, the understood, and to move man to good deeds, even if they run counter to his will. This is indeed religion in its highest form.

Harav Menachem Ziemba contends that a similar situation exists concerning the sociological fact that Esau (the nations of the world) hates Jacob (the Jewish nation). Many reasons have been suggested throughout the ages for the causes of anti-Semitism, yet the causes often appear contradictory in nature and are totally inconsistent. In one country, the Jews are despised because they are capitalists; in another country, the Jews are hated because they are socialists. Here, they are scorned because of their superior intelligence, and there, they are detested because, due to their alleged inadequacies, they constantly present a burden on the community. Some abhor Jews because of their extreme religiosity and others loathe them because they spread doctrines contrary to Christian dogma.

Early German Jewish leaders proclaimed a policy, "Be a Jew at home and a German away from home." They assured us that this would be the panacea that would end anti-Semitism for all time. Yet this policy did not prevent the rise of Nazism.

Rabbi Shimon bar Yochai suggested that anti-Semitism is in the same category as *halachah*. We know of no specific reason for it. It is a blind hatred, and all of Jacob's attempts at appeasement will prove to be ineffective. Some methods may even be counterproductive and increase hatred, as Esau deeply resents Jacob's attempt to ascend to his brother's lofty status in society.

Blind anti-Semitism, in compliance with the *halachah* that Esau hates Jacob, played a prominent role in Hitler's message of hatred. The Germans, unable to explain how a so-called master race could lose a war, found in the Jews a ready scapegoat. Hadn't President Paul Hindenburg's infamous *Dolchstoss* accusation proclaimed that the Jews' stab in the back had brought about the defeat of the German army? The German civilian population swallowed this charge, which had been augmented by Hitler's inflammatory remarks, hook, line, and sinker.

More than two million Germans were directly connected with the Nazi machinery of destruction, and many more millions profited from the pillage and looting. The masses of the German and Austrian populations knew of the anti-Jewish measures. Many were also aware of the ghettos and concentration camps. For a number of years, they heard Hitler and his associates employ the terms *Ausrottung* (annihilation) and *Vernichtung* (destruction) when they talked abut the Jews. Millions of people of German ancestry everywhere in the world became apologists for Hitler's policies.

True, very small segments of the German community did oppose Nazi theory and practice. Certain church leaders were opposed to Hitlerian ideas, and deplored the Nazi acts publicly. Scattered groups from among the professionals, working classes, and former aristocrats resisted Nazi brutality. However, by and large, the Germans as a people did not protest. For years, they heard their brownshirted fellow Germans singing, *"Wenn das Judenblut vom Messer spritzt, dann gehts noch mal so gut"* (When Jewish blood drips from the knife, then things are twice as good), but they did not condemn this bloody slogan of their compatriots. Did the Germans really care about the welfare of the Jews? Most certainly not!

The Nations of the World

DID THE POLES CARE? THEY APPEARED UNMOVED IN the hour of Jewish deportations to the extermination centers. While we bled and died, their attitude was, at best, indifference; all too often, it was friendly neutrality toward the Germans. There were far too many cases of willing, active, and enthusiastic assistance to the Nazi murderers. There was a handful of noble Poles, of course, but nobody listened to them. Their voices never carried above the continual screams of hatred and they could not bring about the slightest mitigation of Nazi ferocity.

The extent of Polish animosity toward the Jews is best illustrated by the Kielce pogrom. After millions of Polish Jews had perished during the Nazi occupation, the Polish masses were still incited by hatred of the Jews. The Kielce pogrom of July 4, 1946 took the lives of 42 Jews in a massacre planned and perpetrated by bigots. This was done at a time when only remnants of Polish Jewry had remained alive and had sought to rebuild their lives in their native country. Although there were occasional acts of heroism on the part of individual Poles who actually risked their lives to rescue Jews, the overwhelming majority of the Polish population manifested an apathy to the Jewish tragedy. They did not really care. They fully complied with the *halachah* that Esau hates Jacob.

Did the Ukrainians care? Did the Latvians and Lithuanians care? Apparently the native populations of those countries regarded the liquidation of the Jews calmly and some even with satisfaction. It is a matter of record that the Ukrainian collaboration with the German units in charge of the extermination program prompted the famous Russian poet, Yevgeny Yevtushenko, to write "Babi Yar," a poem in which he deplored the participation of the civilian population in the mass killing of 40,000 Jews in the ravine of Babi Yar, on the outskirts of Kiev. Ukrainians and White Russians also worked for the Nazis in the death camps, especially in Treblinka. No, the Ukrainians really did not care.

There was, however, compassion for the Jews in some countries. In Belgium, deportations were prevented until the summer of 1942. The greater part of the populations of Belgium and Holland was opposed to the persecution of the Jews. Some of the clergy offered refuge to Jewish children. In France, some Frenchmen in the Vichy nonoccupied part of the country helped Jews to hide or to flee the country. The population of Denmark inscribed in its history a glorious page of heroism and self-sacrifice by carrying out a well-organized operation in transporting almost 7,000 Jews to Sweden. Other Scandinavian countries (Sweden, in particular) made heroic efforts to rescue the persecuted Jews. In Italy, too, efforts were made to save the Jews from Nazi tyranny.

Jews found a haven in Hungary until the Germans occupied the country. In Bulgaria, the population, as well as the clergy, protested against deportation of Jews. In Greece, clergymen in high office and many of the officials not only saved individual Jews, but also voiced official protests against anti-Jewish measures. Yes, some really did care. Unfortunately, such sporadic acts of humanity and compassion were not sufficient to prevent the Holocaust.

President Franklin D. Roosevelt's steps to aid Europe's Jews were very limited. He was certainly in a position to arouse substantial public backing for a vital rescue effort by speaking out on the issues. If nothing else, a few forceful statements by the President would have brought the extermination out of obscurity and into the headlines. But he had little to say about the problem and gave no priority at all to rescuing the Jews.

In December 1942, the President reluctantly agreed to talk with Jewish leaders about the recently confirmed news that European Jews were being exterminated. Thereafter, he refused requests to discuss the problem. He even left the White House to avoid the pilgrimage of more than 400 Orthodox rabbis representing the Union of Orthodox Rabbis and headed by the unforgettable Torah giant, Harav Eliezer Silver of Cincinnati. He declined to discuss the State Department's arbitrary shutdown of refugee immigration to the United States, even when pressed by the seven Jews in Congress. Did Roosevelt really care?

In November 1943, on the eve of his departure for Cairo and Teheran, stirrings in Congress briefly drew Roosevelt's attention to the rescue question. When he returned six weeks later, he faced the prospect of an explosive debate in Congress on the administration's rescue policies and the probable passage of legislation calling on him to form a rescue agency. Not long afterward, he established the War Refugee Board. His hand had been forced by the pressure on Capitol Hill and by the danger that a major scandal would break out over the State Department's persistent opposition to rescue.

The president took little interest in the WRB. He never acted to strengthen it or provide it with adequate funding. He even impeded its initial momentum by delaying the selection of a director.

Rabbis from the Union of Orthodox Rabbis marching on behalf of Nazi-persecuted European Jewry. Harav Eliezer Silver can be seen at the center.

Harav Eliezer Silver leading 400 rabbis in a march to Washington, reading a petition to Vice President Henry A. Wallace to save European Jews from the hand of Nazism.

It appears that Roosevelt's overall response to the Holocaust was deeply affected by political expediency. Most Jews supported him unwaveringly, so an active rescue policy offered little political advantage. A pro-Jewish stance, however, could lose him votes in other sectors of the population. American Jewry's great loyalty to the President thus weakened the leverage it might have exerted on him to save European Jews.

Years later, Congressman Emanuel Celler charged that Roosevelt, instead of providing some spark of courageous leadership, had been silent, indifferent, and insensitive to the plight of the Jews. In the end, the era's most prominent symbol of humanitarianism turned away from one of history's most compelling moral challenges.

David S. Wyman, in his book *Abandonment of the Jews*, writes that "this book has been difficult to research and to write. One does not wish to believe the facts revealed by the documents on which it is based. America, the land of refuge, offered little succor. American Christians forgot about the Good Samaritan. The Nazis were the murderers, but we were the all-too-passive accomplices."

Wyman goes on to say that the U.S. State Department and the British Foreign Office had no intention of rescuing large numbers of European Jews. On the contrary, they continually feared that Germany or their Axis nations might release tens of thousands of Jews into Allied hands. Any such exodus would have placed intense pressure on Britain to open Palestine and on the United States to take in more Jewish refugees, a situation the two powers did not want to face. Consequently, their policies were aimed at obstructing rescue possibilities and dampening public pressures for government action.

Because of the State Department's administrative policies, only 21,000 refugees were allowed to enter the United States during the three and a half years the nation was at war with Germany. That amounted to merely 10 percent of the number who could have been legally admitted under the immigration quotas during that period.

Arthur D. Morse, in his book *A Chronicle of American Apathy*, reached a similar conclusion, when he wrote that "the possibility of mass rescue threatened England's Palestine policies. The vision of Jews streaming to Palestine seemed to upset Whitehall more than the vision of Jews walking to their death in the gas chambers." One might add that not only was Whitehall more upset by such a vision, many other governments were also more upset by the vision of Jews finding even temporary refuge on their shores than by the vision of the gas chambers and crematoria.

In his book *While Six Million Died,* Morse examined the inaction of the American government and concluded that the upright men in the administration of the great humanitarian President Roosevelt knew of Hitler's order for the government's "final solution," knew of the mass executions, but were overcautious about doing anything about it. Mr. Morse indicts the government's bureaucratic delay and its refusal to try ransom and to revise immigration quotas. Thus, through official procrastination, America and England maintained their barriers against any serious rescue attempt.

The fall of Germany, writes Dr. Eliezer Berkowitz in his book *Faith After the Holocaust,* is the fall of the West. Not only six million Jews perished in the Holocaust. Because of the Holocaust, Western civilization lost every claim to dignity and respect. The soul had gone out of the majority of the Western nations. A Jew, familiar with the history of his nation within the context of Western civilization, might well wonder how much soul ever was present in that civilization.

So, did anyone really care? Some certainly did. Unfortunately, however, those in the best position to make a difference displayed little interest. They did not really care at all. That was the true tragedy.

What solution does Harav Ziemba offer to assure our survival in a world steeped in anti-Semitism? How can we combat this blind hatred emanating from the *halachah* that Esau hates Jacob?

In Chapter 49 of his book, he quotes the Biblical verse, "They embittered their lives with hard work with mortar and with bricks" — "וַיְמָרְרוּ אֶת חַיֵּיהֶם בַּעֲבֹדָה קָשָׁה בְּחֹמֶר וּבִלְבֵנִים" (*Shemos* 1:14). The Holy *Zohar* comments on this verse, "The word *chomer* refers to the system of *a fortiori,* which is one of the thirteen methods we have at our disposal to derive statutes pertaining to Torah, and the word *leveinim* refers to the clarification of *Halachah, Libun Halachah*. Through the process of Torah study, concludes Harav Ziemba, we gain the spiritual strength and power to withstand the pain and agony of oppression (as symbolized by mortar and bricks) perpetrated upon us during our years in *galus*.

David Hamelech taught, "Some with chariots and some with horses; but we, in the name of Hashem, Our G-d, call out" — "אֵלֶּה בָרֶכֶב וְאֵלֶּה בַסּוּסִים וַאֲנַחְנוּ בְּשֵׁם ה' אֱלֹקֵינוּ נַזְכִּיר" (*Tehillim* 20:8). Hashem and our Torah are our shields and our keys for survival.

CHAPTER 10
LIKE SHEEP TO THE SLAUGHTER?

WHY DIDN'T THE JEWS PUT UP ANY OPPOSI-
tion? Why didn't they resist? Lately, this question
has actually become an accusation as it points
accusing finger at the victims themselves. These
accusations against the Jewish martyrs have become almost
louder than those against the perpetrators. It seems to be psy-
chologically more satisfying to some people to find the victims
guilty, than to delve into the monstrosity of the crime committed against them. According to these theories, the victims themselves share in the guilt of a widely nazified Europe. They went
like sheep to the slaughter.

Yitzchok Gruenbaum, a well-known radical Zionist leader,
remarked that the Jews died like rags, not like men. In his book,
The Destruction of European Jews, historian Raul Hilberg claims
that the lack of resistance to the Nazis and the cooperation of

the *Judenrat* with the German authorities stemmed from a traditional Jewish policy of nonresistance to oppressors. Others simply refer to it as *galus* mentality.

In his book, *Katzon Latevach,* K. Shabbetai, (Shabtai Keshev-Klugman) himself a survivor of concentration camps, soundly refutes these accusations. In order to understand the lack of Jewish resistance, says Shabbetai, one must compare Jewish behavior with that of the gentiles in similar situations.

In addition to the Jews, there were more than five million non-Jews confined in German concentration and forced-labor camps. All of the nations of Europe were represented among the inmates. The conditions in the gentile camps were humiliating and degrading enough not to be endured by self-respecting people. Yet there were no rebellions and no acts of self-defense in the gentile camps either.

The American Third Army describes the Flossenburg concentration camp as a death factory. Starvation, brutality, medical neglect, exposure to freezing cold, inducement to commit suicide, shootings and hangings, were the methods of extermination practiced in the camp. Prisoners were murdered arbitrarily at the whim of their murderers. All this was done to gentiles, reports Shabbetai. Yet, they never rebelled. They endured it all like sheep.

A most striking illustration of Shabbetai's point is the plight of the Russian prisoners of war. Fifty thousand Soviet soldiers were buried in a mass grave at Bergen -Belsen. They all perished in a manner very similar to the Jewish martyrs. It should be noted that this number represents a small percentage of all the Soviet prisoners of war who perished in the German camps.

Alfred Rosenberg was the philosopher of the German Nazi movement. He stressed Aryan racial superiority and the cult of the great leader. His ambition was to replace Christianity with a Germanic pagan religion. Born of German parents in Estonia, he returned to Eastern Europe during World War II as minister for Germany's eastern occupied territories. He pressed for extermination of the Jews. After the war, Rosenberg was executed for war crimes.

In his missive to Wilhelm Keitel, chief of the German General Staff, dated February 28, 1942, Rosenberg wrote that of the 3,300,000 Russian prisoners of war, only a few hundred thousand remained alive. Most of them had died of hunger or had frozen to death. Thousands more were killed by typhus. The prisoners were shot in full view of the terrified civilian population and their bodies were left lying on the roads when they lacked the strength to continue marching. These were the proud disdainful words of the minister of the eastern occupied territories. Had he no shame?

Polish intellectuals and army officers were murdered by the Germans. They offered no resistance. Likewise, the 9,000 Polish officers massacred at Katyn offered no resistance. Such examples are numerous.

All of these occurrences tend to support Shabbetai's thesis that all resistance and rebellions have their own laws, whose functioning depends on the political, strategic, social, and psychological conditions of the moment. If the conditions required are extant, people will resist and rebel; if not, they will not; they cannot. There is usually no rebellion immediately after defeat; no rebellion as long as the enemy marches from victory to victory. Thus the partisan movement along the eastern front did not really start until after the German defeat at Stalingrad.

The Polish underground was organized soon after Poland's defeat in 1939. It had at its disposal the service of well-trained army officers, soldiers, weapons, monetary funds, and foreign support. Yet for years its main function was to smuggle people out of Poland. In the meantime, Polish intellectuals, scientists, and leading citizens were being murdered or sent to concentration camps, yet the Polish government did not budge, and people accepted their fate meekly.

It took nearly five years after the collapse of Poland in September 1939 before the Warsaw Uprising took place in 1944.

(This uprising should not be confused with the Warsaw Ghetto Uprising in 1943.) And it happened after Stalingrad, after the overthrow of Mussolini, after the Allied landing in France, and at a time when the Russian armies were practically at the gates of Warsaw. Even revolt fears terror and even revolt needs hope. It must have a place to organize weapons and an avenue of possible escape or retreat. These were laws operative all across German-occupied Europe. Millions of gentiles, oppressed and humiliated, accepted their plight without resistance, until the required favorable conditions for a revolt arose.

Now contrast this with the situation confronting the Jews. They were in an infinitely weaker and more exposed situation than all the oppressed people of Europe. The killers were a highly trained army of young, healthy males. They were equipped with advanced weaponry and possessed virtually unlimited mobility. The millions who perished at their hands were civilians. They were either geographically dispersed or were imprisoned in ghettos and concentration camps. These millions included old people, women, and children, and constituted the most undernourished population in Europe.

Once the German armies moved into a country, even the inner structure of Jewry was shattered. The Jew lost his status as a human being as there were no laws protecting his elementary rights of existence. His former homeland became his prison, surrounded not only by Nazi inhumanity, but also by the brutality of the indigenous populations; the Poles, the Ukrainians, the Lithuanians, the Latvians, the Hungarians, and others. Even among the partisan militias who fought the Germans, there existed rabid anti-Semitism. It often happened that a Jew fled from the Germans into the forests, only to be murdered there by the partisans.

Now trapped in their homeland, they were not an army trained for war, not people with a long tradition of warlike skills but men, women, and children completely unprepared for such an emergency. Any possibility of organized resistance by the people in their vast masses, was out of the question. There was no national leadership because there could not have been. Every community, and practically every individual Jew, had to face the limitless ferocity of the enemy in isolation.

Furthermore, the annihilation was carried out using sophisticated psychological trickery. Elaborate systems of deception were meticulously planned and executed. Such an organized, systematic destruction of an entire nation had never before been attempted in human history. The plans for mass murder were, until the end, shrouded in secrecy. The Germans took advantage of people's natural, inherent hopefulness by indicating that not everyone would be sent to the camps. The *selektions* were carried out with suddenness, allowing no time for planned reaction. The mass murders were generally carried out without warning. Many of the victims entered the gas chambers thinking that these were merely showers for hygienic purposes. Isn't this what the sign on the door indicated?

The Nazis also employed systems of collective punishment. A town that rebelled was burned to the ground and its inhabitants executed. When a German was killed by the underground resistance, a hundred hostages would be collected and summarily executed unless the underground fighter responsible for the killing was turned over. In the ghettos, the practice was to murder the family of any person who escaped to join the partisans. Under such prevailing conditions, it is understandable that many hesitated and avoided such a step.

Did we go to our death like sheep to the slaughter? The unforgettable Jewish historian and writer Dr. Hillel Seidman in his *Yoman Ghetto Varsha* (pp. 264-268) emphatically declares no! It is always easy to make judgments when one is sitting comfortably in one's armchair, but it is truly impossible for those who were not there to know what horrors people were experiencing. Thought processes which might be criticized in today's political climate seemed rational and logical then, and it should be understood that the concept of "al tadin" – do not judge your fellow man until you have come to be in his position – is most applicable in this situation.

Dr. Seidman clarifies the trend of thought of the Jews in Europe in those years:

1. Even though they might have heard Hitler and his cohorts speak of the annihilation of European Jewry, they did not believe that it meant actual physical annihilation. Rather, they viewed the concept of annihilation as referring to suffering, persecution, hunger, harassment, possibly even periodic pogroms, but certainly not to total annihilation. They therefore hoped that they would somehow escape, as had so many in past generations. Even when the situation reached the stage of deportations, they still calmed themselves by believing that they were being transported to other locations to work for the German war effort. True, there were those who understood all too well what was happening, but it is not a simple matter to assume the awesome responsibility for the destruction of entire communities by encouraging rebellion.

2. The Germans, with diabolical cunning, hid the enormity of their brutality from the world and from their victims. Often, the "final solution" became apparent to the helpless victims only as they were herded into the "showers." Time after time, we hear of inmates of the ghettos not believing the whispered reports of what was happening to those who had been transported to the East. With the wisdom of 20/20 hindsight it is easy today to say that this or that action should have been taken—but we should never forget just how devious the Germans were in their efforts to hide all traces of their bestiality. Most of the Jews in Europe just did not know the truth.

3. The Jews in Europe naively believed in the conscience of the world. They did not believe that the civilized world, once it found out the truth, would stand by and allow such monstrous barbarities to be perpetrated. They could not believe, once the Allies would verify what they themselves had found out too late, that there would not be a concerted effort to save those Jews who were still alive. When the terrible truth would become known, would any conscientious person in the world rest until the walls of the concentration camps had been torn down? Surely there would be sanctions against the Germans, defense through the agency of neutral states, through the International Red Cross, through the intervention of the Pope...surely Jews would be recognized as international citizens and would receive passports .... surely Jewish organizations, influential men, statesmen, judicial figures, diplomats would somehow act to save them. The poet Alexander Pope wrote, "Hope springs eternal in the human breast." Is it any wonder that these tormented, tortured souls believed in the humanitarianism of the Allies? What is really tragic is how misplaced their faith was.

4. Once the European Jews believed in the conscience of the world, it seemed logical not to endanger oneself more than absolutely necessary, but rather to wait for what was hoped would be a quick salvation. Since Germany was such a major power and since any defensive action caused retaliations on an unbelievable scale, it seemed imprudent to take independent action. Such action would only place innocent defenseless souls in an untenable hostage position.

It should be pointed out that numerous Jews who escaped the German march to the east and were recruited into the Red Army displayed great bravery and self-sacrifice as fighters and soldiers. In the Red Army, Jews received more medals for valor than any other national group. Many of them were escapees from the ghettos and the concentration camps. The Lithuanian Division of the Red Army consisted of 85 percent of Lithuanian refugee Jews. This division fought with great distinction.

Similarly, after the war, many of the physically broken survivors of the camps reached the Land of Israel, defying the British navy and Arab bullets. These very same concentration camp Jews were in the forefront of the fighters for Israel's independence and its defenders, performing no less bravely than their Sabra brothers.

Besides the Warsaw Ghetto Uprising in 1943, there were revolts and resistance in other ghettos and in numerous Jewish communities. Jews resisted hopelessly and fought back, practically with bare fists, at Vilna, Bialystok, Lemberg, Cracow, Bendin, Radin, Brody, Kletzk, Tarnow, Grodna, and numerous other places. There was also a vast partisan movement. The roll of Jewish heroes is endless. Thus, the cowardice hypothesis attributed to the Jews has become untenable. It makes no sense at all.

Is there any *Halachic* validity in armed resistance? Dr. Seidman, in *Yoman Ghetto Varsha* (p. 221), relates that the Gaon Harav Menachem Ziemba once said in a serious tone that there are various ways of performing *Kiddush Hashem*. If today Jews were being forced to convert, and it were possible to save one's life by converting, as in Spain during the Spanish Inquisition, our death in itself would constitute *Kiddush Hashem*. Maimonides even writes that if a Jew is killed because he is a Jew, that is *Kiddush Hashem* and the *Halachah* is in accordance to his words. But today, said Rabbi Ziemba, the only way to *Kiddush Hashem* is through active armed resistance.

It is interesting that Harav Simchah Elberg in his article in the newspaper *Hamodia* in 1984 disputes Dr. Seidman's assertion. He bases his opinion on his personal acquaintance with the Gaon, and on the fact that in the memoirs of Harav Avraham Ziemba from that period, there is no hint that the Gaon actually supported armed resistance. There appears to be no unequivocal consensus among the Torah scholars of today regarding this question. The jury is still out.

There is yet another type of courage and heroism extant in the ghettos and the death camps. It is referred to as *Mesiras Nefesh,* self-sacrifice. Let me just point to a few cases which illustrate this trait.

For some mysterious reason, the Catholic hierarchy of Poland underwent a change of heart and decided to lend a hand in saving the last remaining Rabbis of Warsaw.

There were only three Rabbis left at the time, Rabbi Menachem Ziemba, Rabbi Shimshon Stackhammer, and Rabbi David Schapiro. The Rabbis were asked to decide whether they were willing to accept the offer to be smuggled out of the ghetto.

When the Rabbis met to consider the proposal, Harav Schapiro spoke. "We know full well that we can no longer help the Jews in any way," he said. "However, merely by being with them, we encourage them and strengthen them. It is the last possible encouragement that we can still give to these Jews who are remaining to the bitter end. I simply do not have the strength to leave these unfortunate people." In the end, they all refused to be saved. Only one of the three survived. But not only Rabbis acted in this manner. Many ordinary Jews refused opportunities to escape because they wanted to share the fate of all. For many a Jew, there were more important values to be maintained than the mere preservation of existence.

Consider the case in Maidanek, where a young woman was led out to be hanged in the presence of the other inmates. Together with her sister, she had run away from the airport in Lublin, where they had been put to work. Her sister managed to escape, while she was caught. It was a beautiful day in May. The gallows had been erected in the center of the Commando Square, the victim and the hangman standing beside it. Who helped you get away?" asked the hangman. Her answer was, "A Jewess does not betray those who tried to help her." "Don't you see how everybody laughs at you!" said the German "You are beautiful. One word could save you, and the world is so delightful." She then uttered her final words. "Today you laugh. Tomorrow you will be laughed at!" What a glorious illustration of genuine *Mesiras Nefesh.* She surely performed an act of *Kiddush Hashem,* the sanctification of the Divine Name.

My husband related a similar situation to me which involved *Mesiras Nefesh* in his hometown of Leipzig, Germany. When *shechitah* (ritual slaughter) was banned throughout

Germany, a small group of courageous *shochtim* continued to perform this act in a secret manner, fortunately undetected by the Nazi authorities. Thousands of chickens were thus being slaughtered each week for the consumption of Leipzig's religious community.

Once, a leading member of the Jewish community was apprehended by the Gestapo and was asked which individuals performed the illegal act of *shechitah*. Despite being the target of savage beatings, he remained adamant and not only failed to divulge a single name but he never conceded that illegal *shechitah* was indeed performed. It was yet another beautiful display of self-sacrifice. He did not submit, despite personal pain and torture

What is one to say of the countless Jewish mothers who chose to go to the gas chambers with their children, even though they had originally been spared by being selected for "the *other side?*" How uninformed are so many well-meaning people about Jewish values and the Jews' ability for self-sacrifice. They say that the Warsaw Rabbis should have considered their own escapes rather than remaining there like sitting ducks waiting for the executioner. A culture and a civilization that has spawned the kingdoms of ghettos and death camps cannot appreciate the uniquely Jewish manifestation of *Kiddush Hashem,* the sanctification of the Divine Name, the true face of courage and heroism.

We can only bow our heads in awed silence when we contemplate the mystery of the tragedy of the Holocaust – 'ה נִסְתָּרִים דַּרְכֵי – but after that silence, we must proudly raise our heads again and proclaim to the world: "לֹא אָמוּת כִּי אֶחְיֶה וַאֲסַפֵּר מַעֲשֵׂי יָ-הּ" — "I shall not die! But I shall live and relate the deeds of God" (*Tehillim* 118:17).

⚜ GLOSSARY

Agudas Harabanim .... Union of Orthodox Rabbis

Alef-beis .... the Hebrew alphabet

Aliyah .... the honor of being called up to the Torah

Amalek .... a nation which attacked the Israelites
after their exodus from Egypt

Appell .... roll call at the Nazis' camps

Arba Minim .... the four species of plants
used on the holiday of *Succos*

Ausrottring .... annihilation

Ba'al Korei .... one who reads the Torah at services

Ba'al Tefillah .... one who leads the prayer services

Ba'al Toke'ah .... one who blows the
ram's horn on Rosh Hashanah

Beis Hamikdash .... Holy Temple

Ben (Bnai) Torah .... one who lives his life according
to the teachings of the Torah

Berichah .... escape

Brause	.... shower
Bris	.... circumcision
Chassidey Umos Haolam	.... the righteous among the nations of the world
Chasan	.... groom
Chazal	.... our Sages, of blessed memory
Chesed	.... act of kindness
Chumashim	.... Books of the Torah
Dolchstoss	.... stab in the back
Eidah Hacharedis	.... the Orthodox community
Eishes Chayil	.... a valiant woman
Eretz Yisrael	.... the land of Israel
Galus	.... exile
Gaon	.... outstanding Talmudic scholar
Gehennom	.... gehenna
Gemorah	.... an extended commentary on the Mishnah
Gemilas Chesed	.... a kind deed
Hachnasas Orchim	.... the practice of hospitality
Haeftlinge	.... camp prisoners
Haftarah	.... section of "Prophets" read each Shabbos
Haggadah	.... text read on Passover which relates the story of the exodus from Egypt
Halachah	.... Jewish law
Hashkafah	.... Torah outlook on life
Hashem	.... G-d
Judenrein	.... a place empty of Jews
Kabbalah	.... Rabbinic ordination for a ritual slaughterer
Kapo Kazette Polizei	...........................people who policed the concentration camps

Kashrus .... dietary laws

Kedoshim .... people who gave their lives
for the sanctification of G-d's Name

Kehillah .... community

Kiddush Hashem .... sanctification of G-d's Name

Klal Yisrael .... the community of Jews

Kol Nidrei ....opening prayer of Yom Kippur

Kosher .... food, ritually permitted for consumption

K'rias Shema .... the reading of the *Shema*; when Jews
accept the yoke of the Kingdom of Heaven

Machshir .... one who checks and then
approves the *kashrus* of food items

Maftir .... the last congregant to be called up
for the Torah reading

Mashiach .... Messiah

Mesiras Nefesh .... the act of risking one's life for a purpose

Minyan ...... a quorum of ten men required for a public Service

Mitzvah (vos) .... obligation instituted by the Torah
or by the Sages

Nachas .... pleasure and satisfaction

Navi .... a Prophet

Pikuach Nefesh .... a situation where a life is endangered

Rav .... Rabbi

Raus, Schnell .... get out quickly

Sandek .... one who holds baby during circumcision

Sefer .... book

Sha'alah .... question on Jewish law

Shechitah .... ritual slaughtering

Shidduch .... marriage

Shochet .... ritual slaughterer

Shavuos .... the Holiday of Weeks

Shul	....	Synagogue
Siddurim	....	prayer books
Shtibel	....	small place for prayer; often in a residential building or in a store
Succos	....	the Holiday of Booths
Tatty	....	father
Tallis	....	prayer shawl
Talmid Chacham	....	a Torah scholar
Talmud	....	the oral law
Tehillim	....	Book of Psalms
Teshuvah	....	repentance
Torah	....	the Five Books of Moses
Treifah	....	not ritually fit for consumption
Tza'ar Ba'aley Chayim	....	cruelty to animals
Tzaddik	....	a righteous person
Tznius	....	modesty
Unsere Stimme	....	"Our Voice" — name of a newsletter
Unterfuehrer	....	those who lead the groom and bride to the marriage ceremony
Vaad	....	a committee
Va'ad Hahatzalah	....	a committee formed to save Jewish lives
Vernichtungslagern	....	camps for the purpose of the annihilation of humans
Vierundzwanzig	....	number twenty-four
Yiddish	....	Jewish
Yiddishkeit	....	rules and regulations pertaining to the Jewish religion
Yiddishe Neshamah	....	a Jewish soul
Yiras Shamayim	....	fear of Hashem; conscientiously religious
Yom Kippur	....	Day of Atonement
Zachor	....	remember

Zemiros .... songs sung on Shabbos and Festivals

Zohar .... book on mysticism

Zt"l .... of blessed memory

This volume is part of
THE ARTSCROLL SERIES®
an ongoing project of
translations, commentaries and expositions
on Scripture, Mishnah, Talmud, Halachah,
liturgy, history, the classic Rabbinic writings,
biographies and thought.

For a brochure of current publications
visit your local Hebrew bookseller
or contact the publisher:

Mesorah Publications, ltd

4401 Second Avenue
Brooklyn, New York 11232
(718) 921-9000